"When a Stranger Ca

A Child Development and Relationship Perspective
on
Why Traumatized Children
Think, Feel, and Act the Way They Do

by

Katharine Leslie, Ph.D.

A Guide for Foster/Adoptive Parents and
Professionals
Living and Working With Traumatized Children

Published by Brand New Day Publishing

To purchase copies of this book, send your name, address, and a check for $28.90 (includes $3.95 shipping and handling) to Brand New Day Publishing, 250 Silene Dr., Pittsboro, NC, 27312. Or for special orders contact us at (919) 542-2037 or at www.brandnewdayconsulting.com

Second Edition

Cover design by PsychoCase

Leslie, Katharine
When a Stranger Calls You Mom: a child development and relationship perspective on why traumatized children think, feel, and act the way they do/ Katharine Leslie. – 2nd edition.

Includes bibliographical references

Dedication

To my seven children both foster and adoptive, who taught me almost everything I know about traumatized children. Thanks guys, Mama loves you.

To Steven, my husband and life partner who keeps me sane, grounded, and satisfied. I love you.

Many thanks to my friends, colleagues and family members whose support and contributions to me and this book were invaluable. I especially want to thank my father, Jerome Leslie, who painstakingly corrected every semicolon and comma.

The information presented in this book is based on research and experience. Most of the examples of child behavior and family life are based on a compilation of many different children and families and are not meant to depict any particular child or family. Any illustrations resembling actual people or references to real people were done so with their permission. To address gender issues in writing, I chose to randomly alternate male and female pronouns.

Author's Mini-Biography

Katharine P. Leslie, Ph.D., CFLE, has a doctorate in developmental psychology, a national certification as a family life educator through the National Council on Family Relations, a national certification as a TLC specialist through the National Institute for Trauma and Loss in Children, and is a certified family mediator and the adoptive mother of four special needs children. Her areas of expertise include child development, parenting, parent-child relationships, and abnormal socio-emotional development of abused/neglected children.

As owner of Brand New Day Consulting, Dr. Leslie provides workshops and seminars, training and program development, and research and technical assistance to a variety of agencies and organizations across the country. She's also conducted hundreds of in-home parent coaching sessions for all types of families: the wealthy, the worried, the weary, and the wounded. Dr. Leslie is the author of the book "When a Stranger Calls You Mom: A child development and relationship perspective on why traumatized children think, act, and feel the way they do." And, she is currently contributing to the *Sourcebook of Family Theory and Research* on the topic of "Studying Foster and Adoptive Relationships" (publication 11/04).

CONTENTS

PREFACE

On May 14, 2000 we put our nine-year old family cat to sleep due to renal failure. It came on suddenly and none of us was prepared for her death. Two of my adopted children were present for the ritual (the older two were in residential treatment at the time). Before she died we sat with "Sigmund" in the examining room talking to her, holding her, kissing her, except for our seven year old son. He sat with a blank look on his face, barely touching her and not holding her when given the opportunity.

His behavior seemed odd given he was the one who seemed closest to her; he fed her and cleaned her litter box every day, and she often slept in his bed. He was always kind and sweet to her. He told me that he loved her. But he didn't shed a tear for her that day. Why? Because he had been taught that boys don't cry? "No." Because he was so sad he shut down? "No." It was because he had already blocked her out of his mind. Another day, another loss. No big deal. When I asked him later about his lack of emotion he said "I wasn't that close to her. There's others you know." I had no idea what he meant by that.

Our son was 4 years old when he was taken from his neglectful, drug addicted, prostituting birth mother. His foster mother said, "I'd never seen a child grieve with such intensity and for so long." But when he came to live with us 8 months later it was as if he had built a wall two feet thick around himself. He was done feeling anything. And two years later, it was a rude awakening for us to see that our loving, warm, attentive, responsive adoptive home hadn't made a dent in that wall.

In stark contrast, our daughter (his birth sister), who was two when placed in foster care and four at the time of

Sigmund's death, cried off and on all day and evening. She talked about how unfair it was and how she would miss Sigmund. She talked about the doctors who took care of Sigmund and how her soul was with God. In some ways it was hard for me to cope with my daughter's grief and my grief at the same time, but it was even harder for me to cope with my son's lack of grief. The difference between their expressions of loss cannot be attributed to age or gender, but rather to their emotional health. She is healthy. He is not. She felt grief and sadness, thankfulness and hopefulness. He felt nothing.

INTRODUCTION

In 1996, my husband and I took in our first set of foster siblings to adopt. They were 6 and 8 years old (male and female respectively), and to our knowledge were in fairly good health in spite of being rejected by their birth mother after their father had died several months earlier. We had little information about their early childhood experiences since their mother had relinquished her parental rights without any Child Protective Service (CPS) involvement. Having no birth children experiences, we relied on our parenting histories, parenting books, my education and research on parent-child relationships, and three years of teaching parenting classes for at-risk families to guide our behaviors, attitudes, and beliefs. Six months into the placement we knew something was wrong with our children and like many good parents we blamed ourselves.

We became obsessed with finding a "cure" for them, and our lives revolved around thinking and strategizing over and over again about how to "help" our children. Unfortunately, no matter what we did (changing ourselves and changing the environment), they did not change. Over time their behaviors and our sense of helplessness escalated, throwing my husband and me into identity crises both as parents and as professionals. After all, what good was my doctorate in developmental psychology if I could not relate to my children nor understand them.

In 1998, I had the good fortune to attend a workshop by Nancy Thomas, a twenty-some-odd-year veteran therapeutic foster parent of seriously traumatized children. As I sat with my mouth agape and my mind whirling, I knew this was the tip of the iceberg and I could not even imagine what lay beneath. My husband and I immediately changed our strategies and had the kids "sitting strong" in the hotel room that very night. Our new strategies were very effective in relieving our guilt and reducing family conflict. Nevertheless, the children's underlying behaviors and personalities remained unchanged.

In 1999, one year after our Nancy Thomas induced epiphany, we took in another set of foster siblings to adopt (ages 2.75 and 5.5, female and male respectively). This time we were better prepared for the issues they presented and put some interventions in place upon their arrival. These worked remarkably well in building a loving, reciprocal parent-child relationship with the youngest child, but the older child seemed impenetrable.

That same year during a round of attachment sensitive therapy, my older son (first set of siblings) began to reveal a chronic history of horrendous sexual abuse perpetrated on him and his older sister by their birth Father, birth Grandfather, and a sundry of perverted pals. Much to our dismay, we also learned that he and his sister were still sexually abusing each other and had been since the day they arrived in our home three years earlier. Feeling quite disgusted and embarrassed we now understood why neither of them was any healthier now than they were when they first arrived; we thought we were raising *our* children but it was clear -- we were raising strangers.

I knew then I was heading on a new path in life and I now would be dragging my children kicking and screaming with me rather than the other way around. As you can imagine our family life changed considerably. And, while our children are somewhat emotionally and socially functional (some better than others), we've learned that they have weaknesses and deficits that may never be remedied no matter what we (and the professionals) do because of the psychological and physiological effects of early exposure to trauma.

Since I began to seriously educate myself in the arena of raising strangers disguised as our children (not just in regards to the effects of sexual abuse, but the effects of all kinds of abuse and neglect on child development, parent-child relationships, and child outcomes), I also began sharing this knowledge with hundreds of foster/adoptive parents and their traumatized children. I've spent thousands of hours observing their family functioning, talking to the children, providing in-home parent coaching, recommending treatment options, and creating new theories, methodology, and practice skills concerning parent-child relationships with traumatized children. And, I've educated thousands of social workers and mental health professionals on the subject in workshops and conferences across the country. Although there is still much to learn, I'm considered an expert in the field of family life with traumatized children and therefore writing a book on the subject seems the logical next step.

This book is about the effects of trauma on child development, children's responses to trauma, why children respond in these ways, how their responses translate into family life, and a novel approach to living and working with these children. Trauma, as defined by Webster's Dictionary, is "a painful emotional experience, or shock, often producing a lasting psychic effect." In this book the word trauma refers to recurring exposure to or infliction of abuse, neglect, or chaos (e.g., domestic violence) on children by parents/caregivers primarily during the first three years of children's lives. This does not include normal separation experiences such as parents going out to dinner and leaving their baby with a sitter, or toddlers left in excellent day care facilities for limited periods of time.

The book is divided into four sections: child development within the context of parent-child relationships, parent-child relationships unique to foster/adoptive homes, parenting traumatized children, and therapeutic interventions for traumatized children and their foster/adoptive families.

Two aspects of this book make it different from the many wonderful books already available on the subject. First, by placing the issue of childhood trauma within a child development perspective, I'm able to draw some conclusions as to why children respond to trauma in the ways that they do. Second, by comparing the unique parent-child relationship dynamics in foster/adoptive homes with those of normal parent-child relationships, parents, professionals, and law makers will have a greater understanding and appreciation for the devastating and long-term effects of trauma on children, families, and society, and the immense psychological and emotional toll it takes to raise a traumatized child.

There are some conclusions drawn in this book that were made without the benefit of research, because none was available. It is justifiable and acceptable that this book may be criticized for that reason - it is a slippery slope to imply cause and effect without peer-accepted evidence. Conclusions supported by research are based on my doctoral education in developmental psychology, continuing education through conferences and training with other professionals, my research on birth and adoptive parent-child relationships and parenting behavior, and the myriad books and research journals I have read and discussions I have had with other experts in the field. Conclusions not supported by peer-reviewed research are based on the above experiences and information plus anecdotal evidence from living with seven traumatized children over the years, observations and interviews with hundreds of parents, social workers, therapists, and traumatized and non-traumatized children. I welcome alternative explanations and look forward to reading any research that is stimulated by the ideas posited in this book. For further discussion, contact me at www.brandnewdayconsulting.com.

DEVELOPMENT DEFINED

1) What is development?

We human beings change over time and we change continuously throughout our life span. Not everyone develops at the same rate, but we all follow the same developmental patterns. Many theorists liken this pattern to a staircase. We follow the same steps, but any one person's steps may be broader, shorter, deeper, etc. than someone else's steps. As we climb our individual staircase, the successful negotiation of one step is dependent on the successful negotiation of the previous step, and each subsequent step becomes more complex. We can take a step backwards, but skipping a step may leave us profoundly lacking in some area of our development.

A good example of the staircase is language development. Initially, babies babble in every language on the planet but the sounds the baby hears the most are the ones that stick. Over the next several years these sounds become organized into words, then sentences, and then paragraphs. At the same time young children's words become more understandable and distinct. Their sentences take on grammatical properties of time, quality and quantity, and their paragraphs evoke more precise interactions while conveying more detailed information. Although young children may at times babble like babies, they more often employ sophisticated communication skills.

Incorporated into the staircase are predetermined critical and sensitive periods of development. Critical periods are exact times during which task achievement must occur or be lost forever. For example, vision is acquired during the first four months of life. Should any obstruction prevent the infant from seeing during this time period (e.g., cataracts), the infant will be functionally blind for life. Luckily there are many more sensitive periods than critical periods of development. Sensitive periods are optimal times for task achievement during which mastery is effortless and after which mastery is extremely difficult. Language acquisition is a sensitive period of development.

Language is most easily and most competently acquired during the first six years of life. All children acquire language, even deaf children, so in this regard language acquisition is unstoppable. However, insufficient environments early in life can compromise the quality and potential of language development, and while not impossible to master later in life (out of step), it is extremely difficult and effortful. The same is true in almost all stages of development.

2) What is developing?

a. Physical Development - involves changes in size, shape, and chemical or hormonal makeup of the body (weight, height, gross & fine motor skills). Strength and coordination increase over time, allowing the child to do new tasks.

b. Social/Emotional Development - involves the ability to relate to other people, to learn what they expect from you, how they will react to you, and to empathize with them. This also involves increased understanding of one's own feelings, and learning appropriate behaviors as a response to feelings.

c. Intellectual/Cognitive Development - involves language and changes in the ability of the child to understand the world around her. The child develops categories of things and events that allow easy assimilation of new experiences. Over time, the child learns to talk, read, and think abstractly about things that are not available for sensory examination.

    d. Moral Development (conscience) - involves increased awareness of right and wrong behaviors based on societal norms or codes of conduct.

    e. Spiritual Development - involves the acceptance of a power that cannot be seen but which is greater than oneself. It also may include development of codes of conduct, rituals, and value systems related to a particular religious belief.

3) How does it happen?

    Development occurs when biology (nature) and environment (nurture) interact. Fifty to sixty years ago researchers were locked in controversy as they attempted to attribute certain aspects of development to either nature or nurture (the nature vs. nurture controversy). Twenty years later it was clear this could not be accomplished because nature does not exist without nurture and vice versa. Therefore, all growth, behavior, thinking, etc. is an outcome of their interaction, not solely from one. Seeing the absurdity of their previous task, researchers next hoped to discover how much of behavior, thinking, etc. could be attributed to nature, and how much could be attributed to nurture. Once again, twenty years later, they had discovered another fruitless effort in applying a quantifiable solution to a qualitative question.

    Today researchers are seeking to understand how nature and nurture function together to influence one another. In general, they have found that not only do biology and environment interact to bring about development, but interacting areas of development also function to bring about individual personality and behavior. This book includes several examples of these findings.

4) What is normal?

What is considered normal depends on whether we are talking about science or social constructs. According to science (research), normal is based on the percentage of people that experience, exhibit, act, think, or feel the same way. It is a determination based on numbers and does not imply healthiness, goodness, or morality. By contrast, social constructs that determine what is normal are laden with values; rather than describing numbers, social constructs refer to people's beliefs of what should be or not. For example, science (research) suggests that going to school is normal and home schooling is not normal because most children go to school and only a few are home schooled. However, social constructs suggest that going to school is normal and home schooling is not normal because people believe home schooling is bad for children. This belief persists in spite of research that suggests home schooling has a very positive impact on children, and research suggesting that most people think schools are not very good. Personal beliefs about race, class, and sexual preference also determine what society deems normal even though there are few, if any, facts to substantiate such beliefs.

Sometimes normal is used interchangeably with average, however, that is inaccurate. Normal is representative of a range of possibilities within which most people fall. Average is representative of a single rating after combining and dividing all possible ratings. Far less people fall in the average category than fall in the normal category.

5) Describing Development Systematically

To study anything systematically entails stating a theory (a concept that posits something relevant about the relationship between factors) and then testing that theory to determine whether it is fact. When research supports the theory, others adopt it and begin to use it in a variety of ways. Theories regarding human development usually entail rough estimations of specific times during the life cycle when the capacities for certain skills, functions or behaviors are present. These theories serve as frameworks for examining change over time.

There are four major theoretical schools of thought that are most often referred to when drawing conclusions about human development: a. Stage Theories (e.g., Piaget, Freud, Erikson, Kohlberg), b. Social Learning Theory (e.g., Watson, Skinner, Bandura, Patterson, Casey), c. Information Processing Theory (often neo-Piagetians), and d. Ethological Theory (e.g., Darwin, Lorenz, Tinbergen, Bowlby, Gesell). Stage theories and ethological theories are most often cited in this book because they have stood the test of time and are exceedingly comprehensive in explaining development and relationships.

CHILD DEVELOPMENT

Within a Family Context

Hinde and Stevenson-Hinde (1987) suggest that a child's development is generated by the child and the parent within given situations over time and, therefore, child outcomes can only be viewed within the contexts of their family relationships. This theoretical perspective is taking a strong hold on the field of child development, yet research is still sparse, presumably due to the complexity of the factors involved as opposed to any theoretical weaknesses. Some of the most profound research based on this perspective has been in the areas of attachment and, more recently, early brain development. The research on attachment has been ongoing since the early fifties, and concludes almost unanimously that children with secure attachments with one particular caregiver tend to have more positive child outcomes than children with less secure attachments. The brain research is so new it has not been readily disseminated, but it is strongly suggestive that infants and young children need healthy social/emotional relationships with caregivers for optimal brain development.

If we accept the view that child development occurs within parent-child relationships then it is reasonable to conclude that the quality of the parent-child relationship (positive or negative) will have an impact on child development. The research on attachment and brain development demonstrate this powerful association particularly that positive interactions result in positive child outcomes (e.g., good peer relationships, superior academic performance, and social competence). And, this research has inadvertently demonstrated the inverse -- negative interactions (e.g., abuse, neglect, and chaos; aka trauma) result in less positive child outcomes.

Although the research on the effects of negative interactions on infants and children's brains, child-parent attachment, and other areas of child development is growing; most of the research began by studying what goes right in the parent-child relationship as opposed to what goes wrong, as when the interactions are chronically negative (see Harlow for exception). Even Ainsworth's influential research on children's specific attachment styles did not include traumatized children as subjects. Much of what is understood about the effects of trauma on child outcomes is retrospective and therefore, speculative. Yet, though not heavily researched, there is an assumption in the field of child development that when infants and very young children are exposed to trauma, certain maladaptive trajectories can occur in some or all domains of their development: physical, social/emotional, intellectual, spiritual, and moral.

Examining specific stages and tasks of child development within the context of families sheds light on why many traumatized children suffer from developmental delays and irregularities in day to day functioning, and why it is so very difficult and awkward for them to use surrogate parent-child relationships as a positive context for development.

The following is a summary of developmental domains and the possible effects of trauma. Throughout this book "trauma" refers to exposure to abuse, neglect, or chaos (e.g., domestic violence) inflicted by parents during the first three years of the child's life. Therefore, this section focuses on child development that occurs primarily during this time period.

Physical Development

There are several aspects of infants and children's physical development that are affected by trauma. Physical affects such as malnourishment, failure to thrive, and developmental delays in motor skills, both gross and fine, are fairly obvious, and usually rectifiable. Less obvious are the effects of abuse and neglect on brain development. However, over the last ten years a remarkable amount of research has been conducted on the brain thanks to computers in combination with new and old imaging technologies. For example, CT or CAT scans (Computerized Axial Tomography) measure absorption of x-rays through tissue density, PET scans (Positron Emission Tomography) test for glucose or oxygen consumption, MRI (Magnetic Resonance Imaging) measures the response of cells to radio waves, EEG (Electroencephalogram) measures the amplitude and frequency of brain waves, QEEG (Quantitative Electroencephalogram: brain mapping) analyzes statistically the amplitude and frequency of an individual's brain waves by comparing them to the norms.

From these imaging technologies there is now proof that exposure to abuse, neglect, and chaos negatively impacts the human brain, and therefore human behavior and thinking. This "damage" is particularly profound when it occurs between the ages of zero to three.

Brain-Cement Analogy

Ever write your name in wet cement? It's a fairly easy task. You can use a stick or your finger. You can write just about anything you can imagine in wet cement. Writing in wet cement is fun to do, but that's not why we do it. We write in wet cement because once that cement dries our writing is there forever and ever. So, too, for the infant's brain. If you think about an infant's brain as a glob of wet cement, you can imagine how it has substance and certain properties that make it easy to write in. Now imagine that it takes about three years for that first layer of cement to dry hard as a rock. Now try writing in it. You will need a sledgehammer and a chisel. This is why "good enough" parenting in which parents are contingently responsive, nurturing, restraining, and playful, and healthy environments that are safe, stimulating, and orderly are so important during the first three years of life and why we can not expect future "good enough" experiences to reverse the effects of early exposure to trauma. Those experiences, and, more importantly, children's emotions around and reactions to those experiences, are an integral, imbedded part of their brains. And, like a rut in a gravel driveway, no matter how many times it's filled in, scraped over, or avoided (short of cementing it over), it's baaaack.

Brain Development

We are born with the most brain cells (nerve cells) that we will ever have in our entire life span. From birth on our brain cells go through a developing and pruning process in which many nerve cells die, while more connections between nerve cells (synapses) are formed. Synapses are the spaces between the dendrites of one neuron and the cell body of another neuron into which neurotransmitters (chemical messages) are dumped and exchanged. Receptor sites along the dendrites pick up these chemical messages, shoot them along the cell body, deposit them into the next synapse, and by so doing transfer information from one cell to another.

Each nerve cell (neuron) has the ability to take in and make sense of certain stimuli. Those neurons that share receptivity to similar stimuli will clump together and become connected through synapses. If there are no stimuli there is no reason for those neurons to exist and they die. Hence, for example, infants are born with the capacity to babble in every language but only retain those neurons that are receptive to the language they hear the most. All other language-receptive-neurons die by the time the child is age ten or so. This means that while you can learn a new language at any age, you can speak it like a native only if you learn it before age ten (there are exceptions to the rule, but these would be considered anomalies). Over time the more an infant/child hears a language and the more facile she becomes with it, specific groups of nerve cells will become denser with synapses but will need less of their comrades to do the work of understanding and using the language, which is a good example of the pruning process at work.

Brain Vulnerability

The human brain is both vulnerable and resilient, and it is this way throughout life, but in different ways. For example, compared to adolescence and adulthood, in infancy and early childhood the brain is more malleable (impressionable) and elastic (resilient). This means that if one part of a baby's brain is damaged by physical impact (e.g., car crash) it may be possible for those damaged functions to be adapted by (rerouted to) some other part of her brain. As we age though, our brains become more efficient by pruning out unnecessary cells so that we can do more with less. This automization means we have more synapses, but fewer brain cells, and more determined, less flexible parts of the brain. As a result, there is no room for major adaptation (rerouting) of an entire function of one part of the brain to another part of the brain.

Unfortunately, the very qualities that make the infant/child brain so flexible are also what make it so vulnerable. Because the nerve cells are not yet myelinated (insulated) or connected together with zillions of synapses that would make it denser and more resilient to the affects of trauma, it is susceptible to irreparable damage as in some cases of shaken baby syndrome. Shaking a baby's head is equivalent to sloshing a bowl of Jell-O around inside a Tupperware container - not a pretty sight!

But the brain is equally vulnerable to the effects of emotional trauma. In fact, exposure to either physical or emotional trauma will result in the same three stages of adaptation: (1) shock (decreased blood pressure, body temperature, and muscle tone); (2) resistance (body fights back); (3) exhaustion (body defenses break down due to severe or prolonged exposure; Thompson, 1993). For example, when an infant's needs for food, warmth, and comfort are not alleviated by intervention, the infant feels stressed. To relieve this stress the infant's brain releases certain neurotransmitters (e.g., opiates, enkephalins, cortisol) that temporarily help the infant cope with the stress.

However, if the infant's needs continue to go unmet over a significant period of time (significance is different for each infant) the infant's brain goes into hyper-arousal and is flooded with these neurotransmitters. As a result, the infant's evocative behaviors (behaviors aimed at getting an adult to respond), as well as feelings of pain, are inhibited. Eventually these inhibitions cause the infant to experience homeostasis in fear-induced situations. What's worse, prolonged exposure to some neurotransmitters (e.g., dopamine, nor adrenaline, cortisol) can cause neuron cell death, dendrite shrinkage, and warped receptor sites. In some cases, trauma causes permanent alterations in receptor sites and the traumatized infant's brain begins to resemble that of a drug addict. The limbic and frontal lobe areas of the brain, responsible for reasoning, emotional responsiveness, and memory are most susceptible to these cell maladies.

The Brain's Internal Working Model

Throughout fetal and infant development, "sensation" information is organized, assimilated, accommodated, filtered and pruned to fit the growing brain. It is an inextricable turn-taking process in which intake of stimuli leads to growth, which leads to greater intake of stimuli. All of the infant/child's sensory experiences are stored in memory. Sense memory is the first form of memory but it lacks context and points of reference. Later, between the ages of two and four, in addition to sense memory, the toddler begins to develop autobiographical memory; she begins to remember events as pictures based on times, places, and self.

Some people have a strong sense about events that took place prior to age three or four, but they don't have a picture to go with the sensation. It is an egregious error, however, to assume that an infant armed with only sense memory would not be affected by his environment, as did the mother who told me she wasn't worried about her infant son hearing his parents arguing and fighting all the time because her baby was too little to know what was going on and wouldn't remember it anyway. Unfortunately, the infant's brain is an equal opportunity learner; it does not discriminate between what is good for it and what is not.

Sense memories, whether positive or negative, are organized into an emotional blueprint of responses to the environment. This blueprint becomes the lens from which all future experiences will be perceived, understood, and interpreted. And the responses developed, whether healthy or not, will be the child's first choice in every-day interactions (and the first line of defense). This is called the "internal working model" (also explained in attachment section). For example, a three-year-old adopted child is terrified of taking a bath and of water faucets. He cannot tell his caretakers why he is afraid of the bath or the faucets. It's discovered later that as an infant his birth mother scalded him during a bath. Although his mother, whom he associated with being scalded, is no longer present, the innocuous water and faucet are. And the child, although no longer at risk, behaves as if being scalded is a real and present danger.

A change in environment cannot infiltrate and alter this model significantly. There may be shifts in degrees. That is, the values within the set equation of the working model may change (e.g., feeling more or less of something), but the model still exists. So, for example, this child will have many experiences of not being scalded by water and over time he may become less fearful, but the sense and knowledge that water is or can be dangerous will be ever present.

It follows then that a change in environment will not necessarily result in a change in behavior. In fact, it's quite possible that we should expect the opposite to be true: when placed in a new environment, many of us would rely even more heavily on emotional blueprints, cognitive perceptions of past experiences, adaptive pathways, and habits to guide us in our new surroundings. Any other actions would be too self-consciously effortful (e.g., attending, thinking, feeling, and choosing).

Summary

The research on early brain development has made one fact crystal clear -- infants and children's social and emotional relationships profoundly impact their brains. When children are nurtured well they have optimal potential, but when they aren't, devastating and life-long consequences frequently occur. For years past, and perhaps even today, people believed that children are naturally resilient and therefore would outgrow early exposure to trauma -- that in effect they would "bounce back." But the idea of "bouncing back" should be reserved for one-time traumatic events. Children exposed to weeks, months, or years of physical and emotional trauma will not, and, in fact, many cannot, "bounce back."

Current brain research tends to support this view; the brain is physically etched with trauma. The emotional blueprints in the brains of abused and neglected children were forged through unsatisfactory interactions with their caregivers, interactions that were flooded in pain and suffering as their needs went unmet and their relentless attempts at engagement thwarted. To raise an abused/ neglected child is often like trying to write in hard cement. But the research offers some hope too. The brain's plasticity makes it conceivable that later "reprogramming" by loving, caring, compassionate, and empathic experiences can modify the brain. However, the recipient/partner has to be at least somewhat open to these experiences to fully benefit, and traumatized children are not usually willing participants.

Social/Emotional Development

The research on social/emotional development has shown that the structure of the parent-child relationship functions to produce a variety of attachment dynamics, enhances or deters children's sense of autonomy, self-esteem, and self-concept, and increases or inhibits children's social competence. Less research is available regarding the effects of trauma on these capacities, but those that live and work with traumatized children see marked weaknesses in all of these areas as compared to non-traumatized children. What follows are summaries defining each of these social and emotional capacities and how they might be affected by trauma.

Attachment

Attachment is an emotional tie that infants and caregivers form to one another by responding to each other's needs in a circular correspondent fashion. The caregiver provides a reliable and valid source of safety, security, and comfort (e.g., warmth, food, containment, body contact, familiarity, and contingent responsiveness). And, in response to these actions the infant calms, gurgles, smiles, stares at the caregiver, imitates the caregiver's facial expressions, snuggles in, takes milk, wraps her teeny finger around the caregiver's hair, holds onto the caregiver, prefers the caregiver to all others, seeks to be near and to touch the caregiver, and uses the caregiver as a safe base from which to explore the environment. In response to these positive behaviors, the caregiver's parenting behaviors are reassured and the caregiver provides more attention and loving behavior to the infant, which in turn compels the infant to increase her signaling activities, and so and so on.

Both John Bowlby and Mary Ainsworth have contributed significantly to our understanding of how biological preprogramming of mother and infant helps to foster successful attachment. That is, infants come into the world ready to attach. It is a biological imperative and a survival impulse. Parents too are biologically programmed to attach to their infants, although sometimes environmental factors block their radar (e.g., drug and alcohol abuse, teenage status, history of abuse and neglect, and mental disorders).

The key word in thinking about human attachment, however, is "reciprocity," which is why infant attachment to a parent is very different from attachment to a blankie or a teddy bear. The reciprocal nature of the attached mother-infant relationship entails the satisfaction of needs of each member of the dyad, which is dependent upon their coordinated and complementary interactions. And these interactions affect both the infant's and the mother's sense of physical and mental well-being (see Bretherton, 1992, for a complete review of Bowlby and Ainsworth). Without reciprocity between caregiver and infant, attachment cannot occur.

Attachment vs. Bonding

Although attachment is often used interchangeably with bonding, they are different, though there is little consensus as to how to conceptualize the difference. Bolton (1983) describes bonding as a unidirectional process that begins in the mother as an instinctual desire to protect her infant. Others describe bonding as the end result of attachment behaviors (for one see Bretherton, 1992). Bonding may also be described as what occurs when the newborn imprints on the first moving object she sees and becomes familiar with shortly after birth (Lorenz, see

Fonagy 2001). I find the following conceptualization most practical. Attachment is manifested in emotions and behaviors. For example, stressful situations and separation from and reunion with the "other" activate attachment behavior (e.g., level of distress, level of anger, seeking or repelling closeness, consolability, interest in resuming activity). Bonding, on the other hand, occurs during events in which these emotions and behaviors are activated.

For example, let's say you and I are at a conference but do not know each other. We are sitting side by side enjoying the speaker and looking forward to lunch. Suddenly an earthquake rocks the building, chaos breaks out everywhere and we cling to one another in mortal terror. When everything calms down, we realize we have just experienced a life and death situation that few people can comprehend. Our faces are indelibly marked in each other's consciousness. We share a bit of personal information and after learning we live in neighboring towns we vow to stay in touch. Several weeks after the conference, I call you to ask if you would like to get together and have lunch. You quickly agree and we meet, talk, share, laugh and realize we have a lot in common. We continue to get together, each taking turns arranging our outings. Over time we talk less and less about the earthquake event and more and more about our selves and our shared interests. More importantly, we come to rely on each other for company and comfort -- we are attached.

But, suppose when I phoned you that first time and asked you out to lunch you replied "No, thanks, can't today." So, I try you again the following week and once again you say, "No, sorry, I'm busy." After the third try, I begin to think you are not feeling the same way about me that I am about you. It is a painful realization, much more painful than if we had met at a party, because the bonding event was so much more emotionally intense than a chance meeting at a party. I'm trying to become attached, but you are not reciprocating. Eventually, I give up, probably making excuses like "She wasn't all that any way," but still feeling somewhat rejected and betrayed.

The intimate act of sex can be a bonding event too, and women are particularly vulnerable to these events because they are socialized from birth to connect to others. When they are in dating relationships and engage in sexual activity prematurely, they feel a deep sense of rejection and betrayal when their partners don't call the next day, don't return their phone calls, or break off the relationship. These feelings are much more pronounced than if they had not engaged in sexual activity. If you are with a life mate the sexual act is enhanced and cemented by attachment behaviors. However, couples who engage in sex prior to commitment can find themselves bonded to partners they have no real love for. When these couples stay together, and even marry (because they are bonded), the relationships are highly unsatisfying -- unless they also become attached.

Mother-Infant Bonding and Attachment

Imagine an infant who by way of childbirth experiences an incredible bonding event. She comes into the world ready to use her best attachment behaviors (she initially uses innate/fixed action patterns, i.e., rooting, sucking, postural adjustment {molding}, looking, listening, grasping, and crying). She smiles and stares at Mom. She gurgles and imitates Mom's facial expressions. She snuggles in, takes milk, and curls her teeny finger around Mom's hair. Under normal circumstance, these powerful signals would elicit attention and loving responses from the caregiver that in turn would compel the child to increase her signaling activity.

But what if Mom doesn't respond the way her infant expected or needed? What if Mom pulls away, or doesn't smile or stare back? What if Mom leaves her infant for long periods of time feeling hungry and wet? What if Mom doesn't touch her infant, cuddle her, or play with her arms and legs? What if Mom feeds her infant when she is wet and changes her when she is hungry? And, what if Mom shakes or hits her infant when she cries for physical and emotional attention? This infant is doing all she is preprogrammed to do to become attached to her caregiver, but her Mom is not responding accordingly. Unfortunately, you cannot be attached to someone who is not attached to you -- you can be bonded, but not attached.

There are several variations on the above scenario. Some infants who are born ill and must spend precious early weeks and months in the care of hospital staff can be susceptible to attachment problems, as are infants who don't receive enough mommy time for their personal needs to be met, whose temperaments are a poor goodness of fit with their caregivers' temperaments, or who have multiple transient caretakers throughout infancy. But, anyway it happens, infants who feel abandoned and unwanted by their attachment figures often lose their capacity and desire to try again with someone else.

There is no doubt that some children are both positively responded to and traumatized by their parents. As a result, they are bonded and attached to them and are able to transfer that attachment to others. However, the above stated conceptualization of bonding and attachment helps to explain why so many foster and adopted children mourn the loss of their birth parents and stay bonded to them in spite of all the traumatic things their parents did to them. As a matter of fact, each traumatic experience may strengthen the child's sense of connection to the parent while distorting the child's attachment behaviors and weakening the attachment to the parent. Some researchers and practitioners refer to this warped relationship between child and parent as a "trauma bond." In addition, this conceptualization may help to explain why traumatized children attempt to create chaos where ever they go; their brains respond to chaos with homeostasis, and the chaos creates bonding events in which they can temporarily connect to others without growing attached.

Bowlby, Ainsworth, and most current researchers and theorists believe a secure attachment to a parent is the number one social achievement in infancy, and the most important building block of healthy human development (Fonagy, 2001). If this is true, then mal-attachment in infancy and early childhood should predict a variety of complications in all future development.

Internal Working Model and Attachment

Bowlby described how the infant's "internal working model," developed during the attachment process, is responsible for later deficits if the attachment process goes awry. Four representational systems compose the internal working model:

1) expectations of interactions with caregivers.

2) encoding and retrieval of event symbols related to these interactions.

3) autobiographical memories connecting meaningful events with self-understanding.

4) inferring and attributing behaviors, intentions, and emotions to others; differentiating them from the self.

Fully formed, this representational system makes it possible for the child to predict his, as well as others' behaviors. The system is created when the infant uses the mother as a means to filter the vast amount of stimuli she is exposed to every day. By observing the mother, the infant receives feedback as to her own emotions. That is, the mother's facial expressions, voice, and movements represent the infant's experiences. For example, when the infant cries and the mother reassures her with soft kisses, hugs, and smiles, the infant automatically infers that this is her own inner experience and that she is soothing herself (because infants do not differentiate between self and others). The mother's contingent responsiveness and patterned interactions provide the infant reassurance about her physical safety and also vital information about her own internal state. Later, the child will transfer this into an ability to understand others' internal states (e.g., empathy, perspective taking, and abstract thought).

When an infant does not receive contingent responsiveness, or is abused and neglected, her representational system is distorted and she cannot form a stable and consistent sense of self. She has no means, therefore, of predicting or understanding the mind states of others. Without the capability to accurately know her own mind and infer things about other people's minds, the child will have difficulty learning in almost every venue (e.g., problem solving, understanding cause and effect, vicarious learning, self-reflection).

Furthermore, Fonagy (2001) suggests that the importance of forming healthy attachments during the first three years of life goes far beyond providing safety, stability, security, and a system to understand the inner lives of others. Attachment is the key to "evolutionarily prepared paths" (Fonagy, 2001, pg 439). In other words, attachment is the primary evolutionary mechanism that propels cognitive development and lays the ground work for future exploratory skills, emotion regulation, communication style, ego resilience, social competency, etc. For that reason, being attached to a significant other is not an end unto itself but a means of achieving a variety of other vital skills and capacities.

Hence, one's initial attachment formed during the first several years of life becomes secondary in later childhood and adulthood to all of the skills and capacities it has played a part in developing. This may be the most important point of this book: The formation of a healthy attachment to others during the first three years of life takes place during a sensitive time in development. Therefore, it can be acquired later on in life, although it may be quite effortful. The real problem with not acquiring healthy attachments during the sensitive period is that certain other capacities that must develop during this time (are acquired during a corresponding critical period via a healthy attachment) may be lost forever. Therefore, future potential can be severely threatened when the first three years of development are forsaken.

Unfortunately, it is easy to dismiss the importance of these first several years of life because it is unfathomable that something as simple, automatic and natural as parent and child responding to each other's needs could have such an astoundingly profound long-term effect on a human being.

Object Relations and Attachment

Object relations refers to the capacity of human beings to develop a sense of self in the world through their experiences, and perceptions of those experiences with others. In infancy and early childhood this is accomplished with the primary caregiver during attachment behaviors. According to object relations theory, there are three basic steps to the process of the infant/young child becoming attached and hence developing a secure sense of self: building safety, falling in love with the parent, and claiming and belonging (van Gulden & Riedel, 2000; Winnecott 1948-1971, see Fonagy 2001). Trust is the first psychosocial skill infants learn. When infants are fed and changed on a contingent basis (as-needed), played with, touched, held close and generally responded to when crying, the infant develops a sense that the world is a safe and secure place (my physical needs will be met).

Falling in love happens when the parent and infant begin to share joy, and experience comfort, value and warmth with each other through repetitive three-part interactions: Parent smiles at baby. Baby smiles back. Parent smiles back at baby. Or, Baby coos at parent. Parent coos back at baby. Baby smiles and coos back at parent. Through these types of non-performance based (response is not earned) positive interactions, the baby and parent fall in love with each other and they join the mutual admiration club. Intimacy forms and the feelings of joy, comfort, and warmth are added to the infant's existing sense of safety and security.

The third step is more complex. The child not only needs to feel a sense of belonging and permanency [no fear of "exit" behavior; see section on parent-child relationships] but also must claim the self and the parent-self as acceptable. When the child claims the parent and the parent claims the child, it is a declaration of ownership and acceptance of their natures and established interactions.

Belonging must come hand in hand with claiming, however, or the dyad risks objectifying each other instead of relating to one another. "Trust and positive interactions do not completely form the experience of belonging. To belong is to feel that you will not be rejected -- that belonging is secure. To belong is to experience that all 'parts' of you are OK, that all of you is accepted." (van Gulden & Riedel, 2000).

Stages with in the Steps

To build safety the infant must learn who and who not to trust, and when and when not to trust. Issues of trust are negotiated during the infant's first year of life while the parent and infant are getting to know each other. Initially, they both operate on instinct (not love per se); the parent provides unconditional care taking and the parent and infant attune and mold to each other. H. van Gulden and Riedel (2000) refer to these first several months as the "fog" during which the infant becomes more aware of her surroundings outside the womb and the parent learns to read the infant's cues.

During the "fog" step the parent-infant dyad begin to fall in love and must negotiate their love through several stages as the child becomes more mobile.

1) symbiosis - holding behaviors and prolonged eye gazing cause the parent and infant to lose themselves in the other.

2) differentiation - the infant learns that she and the parent are not one and the same person.

3) practicing - as the infant becomes mobile she begins to separate from her love object.

4) rapprochement - the more aware she becomes of her separateness the more anxious she may become.

During practice the child will check in with the parent after exploring her environment, will instigate chasing games with the parent, and will seek out the parent when stressed. During rapprochement, she may demonstrate renewed dependency and she will attempt to coerce and control the parent and to restore symbiosis.

Consolidation is accomplished during the claiming and belonging step. By around age 4 or 5, a securely attached child will consolidate all of the previous learning experiences to develop a whole integrated self (e.g., the bad me and the good me are both me, and the happy mommy and the angry mommy are the same mommy who loves me). The successful negotiation of this step is "two whole people joined by trust, positive interactions and belonging sustained by the capacity to "hold" the existence and constancy of the other" (van Gulden & Riedel, 2000, pg. 3-36).

Children who cannot perceive themselves as permanent or constant, and cannot psychologically "hold" the parent may become hyper vigilant, attention seeking, in the moment (not able to learn from the past nor accurately predict what may happen in the near future), paranoid, defensive, and unable to shoulder responsibility. This manifests in poor peer relationships, lack of authenticity, and an inability to form intimate relationships with others. They often feel lonely, scared, uncomfortable, isolated, and, strangely enough, grandiose (see section on behavior manifestations).

Children with underdeveloped object-relations-capacities almost never demonstrate untethered, stress-free interest in the world or interactions with others. Their proportional and figure/background perceptions are often faulty (Rygaard, 2002). That is, they often have trouble focusing on or attending to salient aspects of situations and are easily distracted by unimportant peripheral noise, visuals, etc (sometimes resulting in a diagnosis of ADHD). For example, they don't feel danger when they should, but feel it when they shouldn't. They may express little excitement over big events, but a walk through the grocery store causes huge emotional outbursts. They may minimize the hurting of others, yet feel severely persecuted if scolded for hurting others. Additionally, they may only believe something exists if they can sense (see or touch) it.

Ego Development and Attachment

According to van Gulden and Riedel (2000), the flow from a trust in safety, to oneness with the parent, to a separate self safely connected is directly related to the child's ego development. Ego development begins when certain sensory structures are formed through repetitive interactions with caregivers during the attachment process. For a child to develop normally and have healthy relationships with others, she must acquire object and self-permanence.

Object permanence refers to the capacity to sustain a stable sense of someone's or something's existence across time, space and situations. For example, for approximately the first 8 months of an infant's life he will allow most anyone to hold him with little to know distress. He doesn't know yet that his mother is a separate being from himself who exists even when he cannot sense her. He believes she is his creation, not the other way around. Likewise, when he sees his mother hide his rattle under a blanket he becomes perplexed and loses interest. For him the rattle no longer exists because he cannot sense it (see it). Around the 7-10 month mark, the infant becomes aware of his differentiation from his mother and becomes distressed when others hold him or when mother leaves his field of vision. He now knows that his mother is not an extension of himself, but a separate being over whom he has minimal control. Likewise, the infant now looks for the rattle under the blanket because he knows, for the first time, that things exist even when he cannot see them and that they don't exist just for his sole satisfaction.

This rude awakening is both exciting and frightening for the infant who has gained new insight into the workings of the world, but who has also lost some previous perceived control. One could say that this dialectic is the foundation and frustration of the human experience throughout the life span.

Object and self-constancy refer to the capacity to perceive an object as whole across time, space, and emotional states even when the focus is on only one of the parts, or when different parts of the object are being experienced at one time. For example, a child under the age of four may believe that if she wears boy's underwear she will grow a penis and become a boy. Another child may believe that when Mommy gets angry with him she doesn't love him anymore. However, between the ages of 4-6 children acknowledge and accept the fact that boys are always boys and girls are always girls, in spite of superficial changes in their outward appearance. And these children know that Mommy and Daddy love them no matter what, even when Mommy and Daddy look and act mad or express anger at the child's behavior.

According to Kohut (1971), ego development of a resilient self is acquired through an empathic parental environment that responds both to the infant's need for validation of existence and to the infant's need for protection. Parents fulfill these requirements by providing adoration, calmness, and strength. That is, parents respond with genuine enjoyment and approval to at least some of the infant's attributes, functions, and skills, and accept the infant/child's trials and errors as a normal aspect of development as opposed to failings. As a result, the infant/child feels worthiness that later is transformed into self-esteem.

Kohut's description of the parental environment conducive to healthy infant ego development is the ideal. Unfortunately, some conditions exist that inhibit the parent-infant dyad from attaching, which can negatively impact healthy ego development. These include unavoidable conditions such as pregnancy and/or birth difficulties that are medically traumatic (surgery), intrusive (chronic pain) or isolating (premature birth), and infant temperament/sensory difficulties.

More often however, it is avoidable parent behaviors and attitudes that inhibit parent-infant attachment. For example, some people realize too late that subjugating their own needs for the well-being of their children, leaves them wanting; their dreams of family life vanquished by the reality of the responsibilities. Then, there are those women/girls who have children because they want someone to love them unconditionally. They crave the attention society often lavishes upon pregnant moms and their newborns. There are some men/boys who purposely impregnate girls with only feigned honorable intentions because they, too, crave attention and respect from their peers for "conquering the enemy" and for their virility. Still others believe it is their god-given right to procreate while it is society's job to provide for these children when they the parents cannot. Other parental attitudes/behaviors that inhibit attachment include:

1) attitudes about pregnancy (e.g., mother tried to abort, had negative feelings about being a parent, used alcohol or drugs)

2) poor attunement skills (mother is unable to recognize and adapt to the baby's needs)

3) poor goodness of fit between mother's temperament and baby's temperament (mutual sensory disconnect)

4) drug and alcohol abuse (blocks biological directives to care for and nurture the young)

5) abandonment (mother is not present or is unresponsive for long periods of time)

5) chaotic life style choices (e.g., no dependable schedules, no quiet time, multiple caregivers or strangers in and out of the child's environment)

6) mental illness

Parents who are not ready and not able to place their child's needs above their own, who want a child to satisfy personal ego needs, who do not have the financial wherewithal to support a child, and who have little control over their own environment place their children at great risk for a variety of negative outcomes because they may not provide valid and reliable information to the child. Children, who are abused, neglected, or abandoned by their parents, learn to mistrust their parents and, therefore, the world. These children differentiate (separate from caregivers) too early, and then defend against closeness. Because they believe they are not lovable, they defend against any relationship that evokes dependency or love with provocative or distancing behaviors. They fear intimacy as much as non-traumatized children fear separation.

Summary

The sensitive period in development during which the process of attachment can occur effortlessly and optimally is during the first four years of life. The process is long and complex. Duplicating or completing the process outside of the sensitive period may be very difficult, if not impossible. Furthermore, if the process is not completed during the sensitive period, other developmental tasks are at risk of not potentiating. The process begins with the bonding event of childbirth that activates attachment behaviors in both infant and parent. Trust then begins to build as the infant's basic needs for food, shelter, etc. are met, and the parent gains more self-confidence in her/his parenting ability. Hence, the attachment behaviors increase. Next, frequent positive interactions occur between the caregiver and the infant/young child. Onset of positive interactions is not need dependent but nonetheless these interactions are mutually satisfying and therefore strengthen the attachment and the child's sense of self, and the attachment figure becomes preferred over all others.

Contingent nurturing, coaching, restraining, and playfulness help the child build permanency and constancy structures (ego development) that allow her to hold a healthy sense of caregiver and self when out of sensory proximity and in novel situations. Finally, a permanent bond develops in which the dyad is connected together through space, time, and circumstance. Attachment behaviors and ego development mediate the bond, but are not equivalent to the bond (the whole is greater than the sum of its parts).

Secure attachment is achieved by successfully negotiating the stages of attachment within the three steps. While attachments change and adapt to the needs of the attached parent-child dyad throughout their lives together, infants/children who miss steps or stages will have weakened capacities in many other areas of their lives and will find their sense of self severely compromised. If the infant/child cannot perceive the parent as safe, whole, stable, and consistent across time, space, and changing situations and emotions, the infant/child cannot perceive herself as permanent or constant. As a result, the child may live in a state of existential crisis and therefore in constant need of defense mechanisms.

Attachment Continuum

As I discuss the attachment continuum I will refer to "Mother" as the attachment figure for two reasons. First, it is typically the mother who is the primary caregiver (feeder and nurturer) of young children, although fathers can certainly fill this role as well as mothers. Second, for social biological reasons mothers tend to have the greatest impact on child outcomes during infancy and early childhood, while fathers tend to have the greatest impact on child outcomes in adolescence (a variety of research on fathering shows involved birth fathers to have a protective effect on their adolescent children, both male and female, buffering them from almost all major adolescent risk factors {e.g., delinquency, poor academic performance, drug and alcohol abuse, promiscuity, etc).

To say that a child is securely attached, or not attached to a primary caregiver, is not an entirely accurate conceptualization. Attachment is best thought of as existing on a continuum ranging from secure to non-existent. However, current theorists and practitioners are struggling to concur on a shared meaning and verbiage for positions on the continuum. Not to be left out, I put forth the following conceptualization of an attachment continuum for professional consideration.

Given that the attachment process takes place during a sensitive period of development, as opposed to a critical period, and can be affected by interventions, I propose a continuum based on completeness of the process. The continuum would include certain constellations of behaviors separated and placed into subtypes. Completeness of the process could be described as: non-constituted attachment, semi-constituted attachment, and fully constituted attachment. To have a non-constituted attachment, the infant would have had no experiences with the attachment process. Elizabeth Randolph's theoretical subtypes (isolated, evasive, defiant, and bizarre; see under attachment diagnoses) might be placed here.

"Semi-constituted attachment" means the process began, but was not completed, or was sporadically experienced by the infant/young child. Styles and subtypes previously offered, as well as others the research may dictate later, would be placed here. These include: ambivalent, avoidant, narcissistic, role-reversed, and undifferentiated.

Children who successfully engaged in all three attachment steps and are continuing to act accordingly would be said to have a "Fully Constituted Attachment." Although it takes three to four years for a child to become completely attached, many infant and toddler behaviors, and interactions with the caregiver, demonstrate whether the child is on the right path to completion. The following are brief descriptions of the positions on the attachment continuum.

Non-Constituted Attachment	Semi-Constituted Attachment	Fully-Constituted Attachment
isolated, evasive	ambivalent	secure
defiant, bizarre	avoidant	
	narcissistic	
	role-reversed	
	undifferentiated	

Fully Constituted Attachment: These infants are on the right track of becoming securely attached. They use their mothers as a secure base from which to explore their world. They expect their mothers to be accessible and available, and trust that their mothers will be responsive to their signals and communications. As a result of receiving reliable and sensitive care, the infant believes she is effective in eliciting and deserving care. This trust later matures into self-confidence, a feeling of specialness, importance, and self-worth. Typically, the more secure a young child's attachment is to the caregiver, the safer the child feels, and the less likely the child's need to be in control of his environment. He trusts his parent to control it for him. Behaviors characteristic of these infants include:

1) molding body to mother's
2) seeking out mother when distressed
3) not letting negative feelings interfere with seeking comfort
4) obedience/compliance
5) enjoyment of physical contact
6) sustained eye contact

Semi-Constituted Attachment: There are at least five subtypes of semi-constituted attachment, and probably several others that have not yet been identified by research.

Semi-constituted attachment can occur as a result of exposure to trauma or ineffective parenting (i.e., permissive-indulgent parenting; see section on parenting typologies), in which one to many of the attachment steps were either missed or improperly executed. A semi-constituted attachment may result in discipline problems or personality and behavior problems). The five subtypes of a semi-constituted attachment are:

Ambivalent
Infants who are ambivalent towards their caregivers typically need more contact and responsiveness than their mothers are able or willing to give. These mothers are often emotionally fragile, fragmented, and easily overwhelmed (likely a bad fit between infant and mother temperament). There is a huge discrepancy between what the infant wants and what he expects to receive. The more the infant is denied something the more the infant wants it. He needs constant reassurance of his mother's availability and responsiveness, but at the same time does not trust her to give it. Because of his mother's inconsistent or non-contingent responsiveness, the infant fails to develop confidence in his ability to influence his environment. Behaviors characteristic of these infants include:
1) clinging
2) failure to explore the environment
3) whining
4) extreme dependency
5) vacillating between anger and helplessness
6) easily triggered frustration
7) inconsolability

Later in life the child and adult with an ambivalent subtype is often:
1) disorganized
2) passive/aggressive or passive/dependent
3) dependent
4) needy of constant attention/approval
5) incompetent at problem solving
6) life's victims ("I hate you, don't leave me")

Avoidant

Infants who are avoidant towards their caregivers typically have mothers who are unavailable or unwilling to satisfy their infants' needs. These mothers are either neglectful, have poor attunement skills, or enforce their will on the infant. As a result the infant develops a conflict between the kind of contact, comfort, and reassurance she wants and is prompted to seek, and a fear of seeking it. She learns to fear and avoid that which she most wants. This conflict "fuels a fire of cold rage." The infant learns that others can not be trusted to satisfy her needs, that social relationships cause pain, the world is threatening and/or punitive, and that she is unworthy of care. Behaviors characteristic of these infants include:

1) resist physical and emotional contact with others
2) no attuning to own signals
3) low affect
4) anger

Later in life the child and adult with an avoidant subtype is often:
1) hostile/aggressive
2) low moral reasoning
3) apathy and no empathy towards others
4) controlling and manipulative

Narcissistic

There are two other categories of incomplete attachment that I have come to recognize, but that have not been fully researched. One is called "narcissistic" and the other is called "role-reversed." All babies are narcissistic and must at some point recognize and accept that they are not the center of the universe. However, if a mother uses a permissive-indulgent parenting style (see section on parenting behavior) and treats the child like he is king, or she is queen, long beyond the first year of life, the child fails to differentiate between his needs and wants, and demeans the needs and wants of others.

These parents typically hand everything to the child on a silver platter, wait on the child hand and foot, give in to the child's demands, believe it is their responsibility to make the child happy, and rescue the child from uncomfortable experiences and emotions (e.g., consequences of his actions). The child becomes insecure and self-absorbed, not because no one loved him, but because no one ever said "No." The child may have used his mother as a safe base during his first year of life, but he begins to doubt her ability to keep him safe when she does not control him; he perceives her as weaker than him. There may be many positive interactions, but the child never claims all of his or his mother's parts as being acceptable and may never learn to integrate all the parts of himself.

As a result, a sense of claiming is achieved but not belonging, and the attachment process is not successfully completed. The Narcissist believes that human relationships invariably end in humiliation, betrayal, pain, and abandonment. To him, any emotional interaction or any interaction with an emotional component is will end this way. Therefore, getting attached to a place, a job, objects, or even an idea is bound to end as badly as getting attached to a human being. This is why the Narcissist avoids intimacy, real friendships, love, and other emotions. The Narcissist emotionally invests only in things which he feels that he is in full, absolute control of: himself.

Narcissistic children feel insecure about their own abilities while at the same time believing they are better than everyone else. They often fail to learn respect for authority, delayed gratification, or self-control, and they may be very motivated to complete tasks that are self-serving but shun work that is in service to others. They are argumentative and noncompliant with peers and adults, and are generally not very likable. Having never learned self-discipline and self-sacrifice, competency in the art of compromise and negotiation, or the meaning of commitment, they often have unsatisfactory adult relationships.

Role-Reversed

"Role-reversed" attachment is created when the mother believes it is the infant/child's responsibility to satisfy her needs and wants. She believes it is the infant/child's job to make her happy, and she attributes the infant/child's needs to selfishness. She often adultifies the child very early in the relationship by relegating the child to a position of superiority and authority. She will ask the young child's opinion on everything from what they should have for dinner to what the mother should wear. She often confides in the child on personal matters regarding adult relationships and does not protect her child from adult materials. She thinks it's cute when her young child dresses like a teen idol, swears like a sailor, or blushes when seeing the mother having sex.

When this relationship goes to extremes the child takes on the whole role of care taking including abetting the parent's criminal activities. Several examples include: feeding and babysitting younger siblings for prolonged periods, routinely getting mother out of bed after an all night binge, lying to solicitors and helping agents, stealing from stores, and prostitution to support a parent's drug habit or to make mother's boyfriend(s) happy. Unbelievably, I have met children who were expected to perform these duties within the first three years of their lives, as well as beyond.

These children believe that their need satisfaction is always in competition with their caregivers. The only way to gain satisfaction is to satisfy the needs of others, and they must suppress their own needs to do so. They learn a variety of behaviors early on such as deceit, lying, stealing, inauthenticity, stoicism, and protection of those who hurt them. They appear bossy but in fact are just assuming the adult role of telling others what to do and how to do it, and are flabbergasted when children and adults rebuff their "help." They have a very difficult time being children.

Undifferentiated

Infants who are undifferentiated towards their caregivers are characterized by a lack, or collapse of, a consistent or organized strategy to attain need satisfaction. In other words, the child is manifesting multiple characteristics from more than one subtype, hence the undifferentiated/disorganized classification.

Attachment Diagnoses

The DSM-R IV does not provide a diagnosis of attachment problems that coincide with current conceptualizations of an attachment continuum, nor does it refer to established categories developed by research (Randolph, 2002). Instead the DSM-IV uses the classification of Reactive Attachment Disorder (RAD) to describe a child who is unable to form positive emotional connections. According to the DSM-IV, a child with RAD has markedly disturbed and developmentally inappropriate social relatedness in most contexts that was caused by pathogenic care prior to age five. The DSM-IV further delineates two subtypes of RAD: inhibited and uninhibited.

Many theorists and practitioners have found the DSM-IV description and classifications of RAD to be wanting (Randolph, 2002; Rapoport & Ismond, 1996; Richters & Volkmar, 1994). Concerns include:

1) lack of sensitivity and specificity regarding the relationship and developmental problems traumatized children manifest.

2) criteria of pathogenic parenting which may be difficult to prove, and may not be the only etiology.

3) exclusion of other diagnostic criteria such as resistance to drug therapy and traditional methods of talk or play therapy.

4) insufficient subtypes that fail to account for the many variations of the disorder.

Furthermore, clinicians using the DSM-IV could perhaps diagnose the behaviors associated with semi-constituted attachment subtypes as falling under the V61.20 Parent-Child Relational Problems category. Rapoport & Ismond (1996) suggest that this category is the closest the DSM-IV comes to making a "family diagnosis," and although insufficient it covers many of the disturbed interactions that bring children into therapeutic care. To avoid diagnostic confusion and provide clarity to the field in general, future permutations of the DSM will need to show careful consideration of how the attachment and parent-child relational problems diagnoses interface.

Following the attachment continuum, a diagnosis of Reactive Attachment Disorder (RAD) would be defined as an ambivalent, avoidant, undifferentiated, narcissistic, or role-reversed attachment in infancy or early childhood that resists intervention, continues beyond the first three years of life, and impedes normal social and emotional development. A diagnosis of Attachment Disorder (AD) could be made after the age of five if the subtypes persist and are accompanied by: (1) behaviors associated with conduct disorder (CD) or oppositional defiant disorder (ODD), and (2) impediments to neurological, psychological, and physiological functioning.

A diagnosis of AD may be inappropriate for a child under the age of five because so many of the behaviors associated with the disorder could be considered normal during the first five years of life. However, symptoms present during early childhood would suggest there was early onset of AD. In addition, it should not be assumed that RAD leads to AD. Many children maintain their RAD diagnosis throughout childhood without ever acquiring AD, presumably because there is less impairment to neurological and physiological functioning. Randolph (2001) suggests using the AD diagnostic criteria however, for evaluating all aspects of attachment. RAD would be diagnosed when fewer criteria are met and would include attachment difficulties and attachment problems subtypes, depending upon the number of criteria met.

Reactive Attachment Disorder:

There is no standardized tool for diagnosing Reactive Attachment Disorder (RAD). Usually this is accomplished by a differential diagnoses (ruling out other disorders) and securing an accurate history of disrupted or dysfunctional early parent-child relationships. Many practitioners use the Randolph Attachment Disorder Questionnaire (RADQ) to diagnose RAD. However, that is an erroneous use of the tool as it was developed and standardized to diagnose only Attachment Disorder (AD) in children over the age of five. The RADQ can be used if RAD is suspected, but the low scores do not reveal whether the child has RAD or not. Instead, the RADQ will reveal the frequency of specific behaviors (i.e., never, sometimes, often, always), which can be very helpful in directing appropriate parenting responses and in informing treatment.

Children with reactive attachment disorder (RAD) usually have immature moral reasoning that may lead to irresponsible acts. They may internalize shame for existing in the world, but feel no guilt for misconduct, and they are often extremely self-serving and may be predatory. These children have a relationship disorder in which they struggle with getting their needs met in prosocial ways. Although they typically have very poor self-control, they lack trust in others to satisfy their needs and so attempt to control and manipulate others at all times. RAD should be considered if an infant is exhibiting **many** of the following behaviors:

1) does not use crying to get needs addressed
2) overreacts or startles to touch, sound, or light
3) is listless
4) does not hold onto or reach for caregiver

5) has no stranger anxiety past the 10 month age mark
6) has no interest in interacting with care givers
7) does not smile or respond
8) does not track objects with eyes
9) avoids eye contact with people
10) rejects any thing that is perceived to come from the caregiver (e.g., food, warmth, etc.)

RAD should be considered if a child is exhibiting **some to many** of the following behaviors:

1) superficially engaging and charming
2) lack of eye contact on parents' terms
3) indiscriminately affectionate with strangers
4) not affectionate on parents terms (not cuddly)
5) destructive to self, others, and material things
6) lying about the obvious (crazy lying)
7) stealing
8) no impulse controls (frequently acts hyperactive)
9) learning lags
10) lack of cause and effect thinking
11) lack of conscience
12) abnormal eating patterns
13) poor peer relationships
14) persistent nonsense questions and chatter
15) inappropriately demanding & clingy
16) abnormal speech patterns
17) triangulation of adults
18) false allegations of abuse
19) presumptive entitlement issues
20) enuresis and/or encopresis
21) parents appear angry/hostile
22) medication is mostly ineffective

Attachment Disorder:

According to Randolph (2201), a child can be diagnosed with Attachment Disorder if she has RAD plus CD or ODD (suggested by a high score on the Randolph Attachment Disorder Questionnaire: RADQ), brain immaturity as demonstrated by developmental movements and cross-crawl abilities, and other impairments evident through psychological testing. Children with AD have given up all hope that any good can come from human beings in general. They objectify people, and believe others (children and adults) deserve to be hurt like they have been hurt. They are often cruel to animals and younger children, are preoccupied with fire, blood & gore, and are sexually aggressive. These are children without a conscience who show a total disregard for laws, rules, and standards of family and society. They are pathologically dishonest and only gain self-gratification at the expense of others. To find out more about AD refer to Cline (1979), Levy & Orlans (1998), and Randolph (2001). Four Subtypes of Attachment Disorder (Randolph, 2001):

1) Isolated
   a. sadness is predominant emotion
   b. abhor physical contact
   c. people are not available, not able to help, of no use.
   d. omnipotence - I can take care of myself
   e. passive-aggressive, not openly defiant except when faced with needing help

2) Evasive
   a. fear is predominant emotion (particularly of abandonment)

    b. intrusive on adults in body language a
        non-stop chatter
    c. "buy" friendships, which are short-lived
    d. hurting huggers in seeking closeness
    e. can't be loved for who I truly am so I'll be
        whoever you want me to be (chameleons)
    d. never openly defiant, extremely passive-
        aggressive
    f. strive to recreate dysfunctional
        relationship

3) Defiant
    a. anger/rage is predominant emotion
    b. openly expressive - in your face
    c. dangerous and destructive acting out
    d. shortage of goodies and I have to get mine
        cause no one is going to give it to me
    e. isolated or evasive can develop into defiant

4) Bizarre
    a. free-floating anxiety is predominant
        emotion
    b. grossly distorted reality testing
    c. neurological impairment
    d. sensory-motor, learning, and intellectual
        impairment
    e. psychotic thinking shows up in Rorschach
        test
    f. physically odd looking and odd behavior

Other Social/Emotional Childhood Disorders

There are several other childhood difficulties that are often trajectories of, or co-occur with, semi-constituted or non-constituted attachment. Unfortunately, these diagnoses often supersede a RAD or AD diagnosis and therefore, many traumatized children are being treated medicinally, as per these diagnoses, but not for their underlying attachment problems. These disorders include Bipolar Disorder, Post Traumatic Stress Disorder, Attention Deficit Hyperactivity Disorder, Oppositional Defiant Disorder, and Conduct Disorder.

A person suffering from **bipolar disorder** has cyclical episodes of depression followed by mania (flight into fantasy, and speeding up of thought processes), both of which cause generalized performance deficits (Thompson, 1993). Bipolar Disorder (which is often genetic) was once excluded as a diagnostic category for children. However, many practitioners are seeing set patterns of behaviors and affect that cannot be better explained by an alternative diagnosis. It is, however, tricky to diagnose in children and therefore should be done so by a specialist in the field (e.g., pediatric neurologist). Medication can be effective, but it is often a complicated process of trial and error to find the right kind and dosage for each individual. Characteristics of a child with Bipolar Disorder include:

1) hyperactivity
2) sleep disturbances
3) short attention span
5) neuropathology
6) temper tantrums
   a. poor emotion modulation
   b. grandiose
   c. severe reactions to loss

7) moody
8) impulsive
9) obsessive
10) learning inhibitions
11) antisocial
   a. controlling
   b. demanding
   c. histrionic quality

Post Traumatic Stress Disorder (PTSD) can result from witnessing or experiencing violence, abuse, neglect, and/or chaos. PTSD is different from paratactic distortions. Paratactic distortions come from misperceived sensory input that triggers a survival response as if the danger were occurring at that moment. A child experiencing a paratactic distortion believes that current caregivers are dangerous and that she is being hurt right now when she is not. PTSD includes generalized anxiety in response to a traumatic event, recollection of images of a traumatic event, either consciously or in dream states, and intense distress when internal or external cues symbolize the event. Characteristics of a child with PTSD include:

1) triggers reminding child of the trauma
2) fearfulness
3) numbing of responsiveness
4) isolation
5) sleep disturbances
6) night terrors
7) avoidance of reminders of trauma
8) hyper-arousal
9) difficulty concentrating
10) anxiety
11) emotional detachment
12) aggressiveness

Aggressive or "Externalizing" Disorders are diagnosed when a core set of negative, defiant, or hostile behaviors are present consistently over a period of time. According to the DSM-IV these include ADHD, ODD, and CD. In all of these cases medication can be used to control behavior, but it does not eliminate the disorder.

1) Attention Deficit Hyperactivity Disorder (ADHD) is most often caused by a physiological problem; environmental (e.g., permissive parenting) and social factors correlate but are not causal factors. A child diagnosed with ADHD has behavioral and learning difficulties relating to inattention, impulsivity, and hyperactivity. No one treatment alone has demonstrated effectiveness in remediating this condition. However, medication in combination with behavior modification and changes in the environment appears to be an effective treatment plan. Sometimes traumatized children are diagnosed with ADHD when the real culprit is RAD (either coexisting with ADHD or exclusively present). In these cases, parents and teachers may notice a slight dampening effect from medication, but the social/emotional problems associated with RAD are for the most part unresponsive to drug therapy. A child who truly suffers from ADHD, however, will usually respond quite remarkably to drug therapy.

2) Oppositional Defiant Disorder (ODD) is often diagnosed when the child has strong negative responses to authority figures, limit setting, and expectations of compliance. The child can exhibit these negative responses at home or in school, and sometimes in both places. Characteristics of a child with ODD include:

a. aggressive
b. emotional
c. disruptive
d. controlling/coercive
   coping strategy

e. poor problem solving skills
f. Impulsive
g. initiator of conflict

3) Conduct Disorder (CD) is ODD plus antisocial thinking and behavior. It is exhibited in every environment (at home and at school). CD is often a precursor to Personality/Character Disorder or Antisocial Personality Disorder in adulthood.

Characteristics of a child with CD include:

- a. unreliable
- b. irresponsible
- c. lack of conscience
- d. dishonest/pathological lying
- e. self-gratification at the expense of others
- f. feelings of unworthiness
- g. disregard for laws, rules, & standards of family & society.

Other possible diagnoses include Adjustment Disorder and conditions associated with Anxiety Disorders. For a description of childhood disorders see *DSM-IV Training Guide For Diagnosis of Childhood Disorders* by Rapoport and Ismond; *Help For the Hopeless Child* by Ronald Federici.

Social Emotional Development Continued

Many researchers and practitioners agree that becoming attached is the first developmental task and the fundamental building block of all current and future relationships and potential learning. It follows that trauma would have a profound impact on this developmental task. But trauma impacts other developmental tasks as well. We turn now to the impact of trauma on social and emotional development other than attachment, and the impact of trauma on cognitive and moral development as well.

Autonomy, Shame and Guilt

To say that one is autonomous is to say that one is independent (able to act alone) and able to govern (control) oneself. There is debate as to when the striving for autonomy actually begins, where it ends, and the domains in which autonomy is asserted, but it is first observable during early childhood when increased mobility, verbal skills, and control over bodily functions allow the toddler to gain personal authority over the self.

The young child's striving for autonomy is accompanied by an uneasy sense of uncertainty as his need to be separate competes with his need to merge with others. During the autonomy stage this often looks like a battle of wills as the child challenges parental power to achieve independence. But, the child does not gain a healthy sense of self by winning this battle. The more lenient the parent the more likely the child will engage in rebellion to abolish the parent's power all together. On the other hand, the better the parents are at controlling, initiating, and educating the child, the stronger and healthier the child's self becomes. The child learns to sacrifice a part of his autonomy to feel secure and connected.

This process, however, is not accomplished without some very strong emotions, the most prevalent being shame and, later on, guilt. For example, a toddlers biological urge to explore her world is so strong, she will suffer some dehumanizing interactions (according to her perceptions) to satisfy this urge, as when poised at the electrical socket readying a finger for the shock of her life, and you yell "Stop, get away from there." Your vehemence, anger, and disapproval cause your toddler to dissolve into tears with an expression of incredulity and shame as if thinking, "How could you talk to me that way. You have cut me to the core. You must hate me. I must be the worst person in the world."

Shame is about the whole self and the young child can not yet think in "parts" language (object relations theory; able to separate behavior from the self). When the child misbehaves she experiences chastisement as condemning of her whole self, placing the child in existential crisis. Sometimes the child will lash out physically in retaliation against you, the person she believes is causing her to feel this way. But as you soon begin to hug, kiss, and pleasantly attend to your child once again all is forgotten and she is once again the beloved, good child. You have in fact helped your child modulate and shift emotion states; that is, until the next limit-setting event. And although your toddler is initially confused by this incongruence (how can I be this horrific human being if mom still loves me?), over time and many thousands of appropriate limit-setting events later, your toddler learns to integrate her own needs and wants with yours, and in so doing reconciles feelings of shame and acquires self-control. When this occurs, the child will still experience shame for wrongdoing but it will not overwhelm her and she will be able to shift emotion states on her own and into a higher level of responsibility through feelings of guilt.

Guilt is a more complex emotion than shame. Others can make you feel ashamed just for existing in the world, but guilt is something we must place on ourselves for wrongdoing. According to Erikson (1963) young children must reconcile feelings of guilt with their desire to take initiative because sometimes their initiatives cause problems for other people. For example, when taking initiative results in breaking Mommy's favorite vase, guilt triggers a sense of sadness in the child and a desire to repair the damage his behavior has caused. But moreover, guilt entails acknowledging his own fallibility while at the same time accepting that one who is fallible is still lovable. If a parent rarely acknowledges a child as being both fallible and loveable, the child cannot imagine it to be true and will remain overwhelmed with feelings of worthlessness and guilt.

The process of gaining autonomy is continually played out within the parent-child relationship as they negotiate and renegotiate to strike a balance between the child's and the parent's areas of discretion. Sometimes this process is balanced and harmonious, as when the child's attempts at autonomy are managed well by the parent and the results benefit both child and parent. Sometimes the process is imbalanced and discordant, as when the child overestimates his or her limits and rights, and/or the parent underestimates the child's emotional competencies and needs and/or overestimates the child's physical and cognitive competencies and needs.

However, sometimes the process is so imbalanced and discordant that it is in fact traumatizing to the child, as when the parent regularly takes advantage of, devalues, or punishes the child's competencies, biological processes (e.g., defecation), or needs (e.g., hunger). In this case, the child receives irrational negative feedback for his urges and actions and often does not receive the subsequent hugs and kisses that relieve the shameful feelings and assure the child he is still worthy of love.

Feelings of shame cause a child tension and worry and the child often responds with avoidance of the situation and anyone associated with having caused the feeling. However, excessive feelings of shame (caused by parental criticism, withdrawal of praise, or humiliation) flood the child with a profound sense of worthlessness and prime her for adopting an unhealthy internal working model. For example, a child confronted with such parental assaults often shifts the meaning of these assaults (e.g., denies, disavows, negates, etc.) to prevent a reactive state of rage or a ubiquitous sense of helplessness and disorientation. These shifts in meaning permit the child to reduce her sense of "badness" and exaggerate her sense of control. Unfortunately, this internal working model prevents the child from successfully integrating acceptable shameful feelings into perceptions of the self, and from taking the next developmental stair step - that of facing responsibility, and when failing, assuming guilt.

Shame and guilt are important cornerstones to a civilized society as they demonstrate concern for ourselves and for other human beings. The right amount of shame motivates people to take action, and the right amount of guilt stops people from taking action. However, too much or too little shame and guilt dictates mental instability. Excessive shame inhibits one from loving others and is characteristic of homicidal or sadistic tendencies, while excessive guilt inhibits one from loving himself and is characteristic of suicidal or masochistic tendencies. On the other hand, excessive shame and deficient guilt are characteristics of borderline and narcissistic personality disorders (Gilligan, 1999).

James Gilligan's studies on the minds and motives of heinous criminals show these men to have a tremendous sense of shame for existing, and absolutely no feelings of guilt for doing. Their shame ethics encompass a belief that others are evil and dangerous to them and therefore deserve the punishments that they, the criminals, inflict. Not surprisingly, almost all of these men were victims of childhood trauma (Gilligan, 1999). Gilligan surmises that violence is the male response to overwhelming feelings of shame (90% of homicides and 80% of suicides are committed by males).

The behaviors of many traumatized children stem from overwhelming feelings of shame, or guilt, or both. Those overwhelmed with shame and deficient in guilt work towards righting the wrong that was done to them, as opposed to assuming responsibility for their actions. As a result nothing is ever their fault, and they are almost pathologically obsessed with being right, or never being wrong. According to Randolph (2001), never being wrong is the only way for some traumatized children to feel loved because feeling loved by being right, approved of, or accepted was not available. Those traumatized children overwhelmed with guilt have tremendous learned helplessness and tend to assume that everything is their fault and nothing will turn out right. They are often passive/aggressive, very insecure, and negative.

Research has not yet demonstrated what factors determine which traumatized children will exhibit excessive shame and which will exhibit excessive guilt.

However, it is likely that children's temperaments, the type of trauma they experienced, and the point in their development when the trauma occurred all play a role.

Self-Esteem and Self-Concept

Self-esteem is defined as finding pleasure, satisfaction, and love in different parts of the self, the parts being one's self-concept. Self-concept then is "who you are" and self-esteem is "how you feel about who you are." Of course, we are not always happy and pleased with every part of who we are, but the broader the self-concept, the more possibilities for self-esteem. The process of acquiring self-esteem is initiated in infancy, when love, acceptance, and value are given to the infant unconditionally just for existing in the world. This unconditional love and acceptance experienced in the first year or two of life lays the foundation for later self-esteem. As the child ages, however, the criteria and conditions for acceptance change -- existence alone is no longer enough. In other words, a mother may love her child just for being, but everyone else will expect something from the child.

These new expectations cause the child to have many self-doubts, but with a foundation of self-esteem and a broad self-concept (the self is multifaceted), the child can most likely weather the criticism and negative evaluations that usually accompany socialization into the larger community. With increasing age, children further internalize the criteria (standards to be attained) for positive self-esteem and begin to evaluate themselves against these external criteria. This social comparison can spur children on to greater achievements, which serves to broaden their self-concept and strengthen their self-esteem. And thus a parent's unconditional adoration of the infant and later expectations for prosocial behaviors create a psychological loop within the child by which he satisfies the expectations of others, is reinforced by others, internalizes their acceptance, and satisfies expectations within himself, which then gives him impetus to satisfy the expectations of others, and so on. The positive actions and emotions of the parent early in the child's existence help to create within the child a functional system for gaining a robust sense of self and a sense of belonging to the larger community.

However, those infants and very young children who infrequently, or never, feel a deep sense of being loved, accepted, and valued by significant others never learn to love, accept, and value themselves. There is no esteem by others to internalize into self-esteem. As a result, no psychological loop of prosocial behaviors, and no sense of reward for doing so are initiated. Therefore, no functional system is created. Those children whose feelings of self-doubt and worthlessness are anchored in shame create rich fantasy lives of false attributes, unearned pride, and omni-innocence. These children often don't wait to receive accolades from others, but, instead, are self-congratulatory for the simplest of deeds and offended when others don't think equally as highly of them. In essence, they continue to function as if they should be loved, admired, and exalted just for existing in the world.

Other traumatized children's fantasy lives take on a more bleak and desperate appearance. Their feelings of self-doubt and worthlessness are anchored by guilt and they assume they are unlovable and that no one can, or ever will, love them. Their sense of being unlovable internalized as self-loathing, which immobilizes them and cripples their development. Depression and self-abuse are common responses. To maintain this negative working model, these children will take on life-long crusades to prove to everyone that they are unlovable. This usually includes sabotaging all good that comes their way, leeriness and negativity about trying new things, and lack of mastery. Conveniently, if there is no self-concept then there is no need for self-esteem

Most people assume that low self-esteem is a correlate of negative and self-defeating behaviors. The lower the self-esteem the more likely the individual will be unhappy and behave in antisocial ways. And this may be true in some cases. Interestingly, however, there seems to be a perversion of this negative correlation within the criminal population. Gilligan (1999) discovered that heinous criminals have unrealistically high self-esteem (inflation of strengths and self-importance, and denial of weaknesses) that bares no relationship to their actual behaviors. It appears then that, high levels of shame coupled with low levels of guilt and inflated self-esteem form a correlative triad to criminal behavior.

Social Competence

Children who are well balanced in their sense of autonomy and belonging, and who have realistic self-esteem, are typically socially competent. That is, they not only get along well with peers but can also successfully navigate novel social situations. One definition of social competence is the achievement of a balance between pursuing one's own personal goals while respecting the rights of others to pursue their own personal goals (Crockenberg, Jackson, & Langrock, 1996). The trick to this balancing act is the recognition that one's own goals may conflict with the goals of others and that to achieve fair outcomes for all requires skills to accommodate both individual goals and mutual goals (Crockenberg, et al., 1996). The parent-child relationship provides many opportunities for learning social competence because parents have more advanced social skills to teach competence, and the nature of the relationship offers repeated occasions to experience conflicts of interest. Thus, when parents and children resolve their conflicts collaboratively, both receive complementary or corresponding outcomes. The children, by practicing collaboration with their parents, are more likely to become socially competent.

However, if the child's goals are never satisfied (as is the case with many traumatized children), or are continuously relegated to the back burner, if it was always the parents' way or the highway, if complementary or corresponding resolution was never an outcome, then the child never learns to balance the pursuit of her own personal goals with the rights of others to pursue their own personal goals. As such, the child believes that her goals are the only ones that count. Negotiation and compromise are not acceptable problem-solving options because they will result in failure to achieve the goal. And, if the child's personal goal achievement is thwarted in any way, the child may lash out with a variety of defending behaviors such as blaming others, false allegations, prolonged tantrums, and/ or violence.

Play

Self-understanding is facilitated by social context and the most important of these for the infant and young child is play. Over 70 years ago, Parten's (1932) observations of young children's play behaviors were separated into five categories that are still relevant today.

Onset of the first four categories occurs during the first five years of life. However, all of the play behaviors are apparent throughout development; we don't out grow them.

1) "Solitary" play - child is absorbed in his own movements and is oblivious to others around him.

2) "Onlooker" play - child watches others, is often hesitant to join in, but is learning vicariously.

3) "Parallel" play - children play similarly and are in the same location but are not interacting and pay little attention to each other; also called sandbox play.

4) "Associative" play - children interact but not in any cohesive manner; also called silly play; they may share, get physical with each other (rough and tumble) or chatter incessantly at each other (language play). Their goal is to connect with each other but not necessarily to accomplish any joint goal.

5) "Cooperative" - children are willing and able to work towards a common goal; they can agree to a set of rules and roles, and enjoy the structure of games and organized sports; they are usually able to play cooperatively by age eight.

Within each of these play categories the child can act either destructively or constructively. Usually, children are in destruct mode prior to age six, and move into construct mode after age six. Being destructive takes initiative, but no particular skill. Conversely, being constructive takes mastery, which involves many skills and brain-power (e.g., concentration, tenacity, thinking, planning). For example, an eight year old creates a tower with blocks. He works long and hard on it, sorting the colors just so, keeping it straight and tall, and using every block available. This child feels good about his accomplishment. Then, his three-year-old sister walks into the room, sees the block tower and takes a running header into the middle of it before her brother can stop her. She laughs and screams with excitement as the blocks fall down around her. Her brother, on the other hand, dissolves into a puddle of tears. The three year old is not being bad. She is taking the developmental steps necessary to achieve what her brother already has -- children usually must learn to destruct something before they can learn to construct something.

Social play provides the context within which more complex and mature skills are learned. The more the child plays, and the more diverse play categories the child engages in, the more socially competent and self-knowledgeable the child becomes. Unfortunately, because traumatized children's interpretation/ perception of the social context is often negative, they do not use it as a means of self-discovery through play. This most often results in arrested play development. Traumatized children are usually stuck in associative play and destruct mode. These children most often distract and detract from play interactions. They don't join in to pre-existing play groups, and instead attempt to lure children to them with a different activity. When this fails, they will initiate associative play, by acting silly or annoying.

It often appears that these children would rather receive negative than positive attention. This may be true, but it is also likely the child does not trust the positive attention because it does not fit his negative working model. Positive attention may be interpreted as, "What does this person want from me?" Alternatively, some of these children do not even notice that anyone is even paying attention to them, negatively or positively because they are parallel playing. For example, a child described by her teacher as attention seeking because she is climbing on her desk at school may actually not have any perception that anyone is watching her but is simply entertaining herself.

Traumatized children stuck in associative play are usually controlling of all play activity and prefer to play with younger children who are more likely to follow along. The older the child, the more problematic his destruct mode becomes as he destroys his own toys under the guise of taking them apart and fixing them. Unfortunately, these children can take things apart, but they usually cannot reconstruct them. They often show no mastery of specific activities because (1) they don't believe that they can master them, (2) it's easier and more rewarding to fantasize that they can or have mastered them then to actually try, and (3) even if they could master them they don't see the purpose. Structured games with rules and roles are seen as boring. Chaos is the only game in town - no rules, no expectations, and they can always claim to have won. Also, if the child really wants to be controlling he'll make up his own game and rules, and mete out the winning hands as he sees fit.

Empathy

Empathy is the vicarious sensation of someone else's emotional state or condition. In many cases, showing empathy entails spontaneous helping, sharing, or comforting behaviors, and sometimes temporary self-sacrifice for the benefit of another. Some researchers claim that we are born with an empathetic distress reaction that becomes more sophisticated with maturation and social cognition, and, that is heavily mediated by family environments (Sagi & Hoffman, 1976). For example, research has shown that healthy, attached infants cry when other infants cry, demonstrating "global" empathy. And, children as young as two years of age can use "egocentric empathy" to soothe another child who is in distress (e.g., giving one's own pacifier, toy, or blanket to another child who is crying: "Hey it works for me, maybe it will work for you.") (Eisenberg & Mussen, 1989).

Empathy for another's feelings emerges between the ages of four to six when children recognize that others' feelings may be different from their own. And, late in childhood, empathy for another's life condition is experienced when children are able to make elaborate appraisals of another's situation because of their greater understanding of social concepts and contexts (e.g., poverty, wealth, divorce, death, freedom).

But many abused infants and young children react quite differently to distressed children than those who have not been abused. Some abused children show no reaction to their distressed counterparts, others show fear and hide from the distressed child, covering their ears to block out the crying. Still, others actually threaten or hit the distressed child to make the child stop crying (Main & George, 1985). In other words, abused children's understanding, sensitivity, and responsiveness to another's feelings are warped. Unfortunately, this has long-term effects. School age is a time when feelings of empathy should be increasing, but the abused child becomes more isolated and aggressive. School-aged children who rate low on empathy scales by their peers are more likely to be rejected by their peers and to adopt antisocial roles. On the other hand, those children who score high on empathy rating scales are more likely to have affectionate parents and a strong obligation to caring for immediate family members (Eisenberg & Mussen, 1989).

Cognitive Development

Cognition can best be described as processes of knowing and learning. According to Piaget's Theory of Cognitive Development human beings innately strive to balance experience with the ability to understand and explain that experience. Hence knowing and learning naturally occurs. During the first eight years of development, play is the primary mode of knowing and learning. During the next eight years, problem - solving practical and every day experiences - is the primary mode of knowing and learning, although children still play. In adulthood theoretical problem solving becomes an important mode of knowing and learning, although adults still play and problem solve every day experiences.

Piaget established four stages of cognitive development still widely accepted today. During the first two years of life, infants and toddlers are said to be in the Sensory Motor stage of development during which they have the capacity to create meaning through their senses (i.e., sight, sound, touch, smell, taste). Between ages two and six, children are said to be in the Preoperations stage of development during which they have the capacity to create meaning through fantasy. Between ages seven and eleven, older children are said to be in the Concrete Operations stage of development during which they have the capacity to create meaning from reality. Beginning around age twelve, and continuing throughout adulthood, the Formal Operations stage of development allows us to create meaning from thought without the benefit of sensory input. That is, we can speculate, theorize, and deduct from sources that are not readily available for examination; we can think, "If this, then that," even if we have never experienced the this or the that.

Piaget suggested that human beings are biologically programmed for these developmental stages to unfold during sensitive periods, in succession, over time. He also suggested that a "good enough" environment was necessary for the successful completion of each cognitive task and that attainment of formal operations was not likely to be completed without the presence of specific environmental stimulants (e.g., significant problem solving opportunities plus theoretical discussions during adolescence).

All interactions with more competent adults, siblings or peers can provide learning opportunities for children. However, parent-child interactions provide the first, the predominant, and the most salient environment for cognitive development to take place (Vygotsky, 1929 - 1978; Maccoby, 1992). Vygotsky likens these interactions to a building scaffold. The scaffold surrounds the building, but is not the building itself, nor is it incorporated into the building; the building is erected step by step with the support of the scaffold.

Imagine a young child learning to read over a period of months or years. The parent first reads to the young child, later points to the words and sounds them out, and then when the child shows readiness has the child repeat the words. Eventually, the child sounds out the words with the parent's help. When the child begins to read independently the parent assists and corrects when needed. The child's "reading building" is erected over time, step by step from the ground up with the parent's support. The parent provided authority and knowledge that continually adjusted to the child's knowledge and abilities until independence and mastery were achieved. These scaffolding interactions enable children to reach higher levels of cognitive functioning (within certain parameters {e.g., maturation}).

Interestingly, but not surprisingly, traumatized children suffer more often from cognitive malfunctioning and distortions than non-traumatized children, presumably because their processes of knowing and learning are skewed from on-going interactions with abusive partners, or partners who are no more competent in problem solving then the children are themselves.

The potential for cognitive malfunction begins when sensory input is distasteful, doesn't fit the child's needs, or is chaotic on a consistent basis. Early exposure to trauma (e.g., not being fed, bathed, changed, clothed on a regular schedule) may prevent the infant's brain from assimilating and accommodating information into organized patterns necessary for complex learning abilities. Also, when the brain is immature, sensory input is primarily filtered through the midbrain regions (the defense mechanism zone, i.e., freeze, flight, or fight) with little input from the frontal lobe (reasoning and problem solving zone). Exposure to trauma causes over-development of the midbrain, which then may resist mediation from future frontal lobe input (Perry, 1995). And, if the frontal cortex is not engaged, anything more than procedural learning is not occurring

For example, Gacono and Meloy (1994) found that sexually abused children's thinking, as measured by responses to the Rorschach projective ink blot test, more closely resembled that of schizophrenics than that of non-sexually abused children. And, in general, they found that abused and neglected children adopt more disassociative defenses (e.g., extensive fantasizing, thinking errors, and misinterpretations of social cues) than non-abused or neglected children.

Preoperational abilities may bring some relief to trauma experiences as they allow children to fantasize that they are omnipotent and invulnerable. However, many foster and adoptive parents describe traumatized children in ways that suggest they are very smart but seem to be arrested at the preoperational stage. I assume this is because imagining omnipotence and invulnerability works so well at relieving the stress of being traumatized that it often turns into a belief system. Because human beings are driven toward certainty (to resist stress) they will impose patterns on unpatterned stimuli -- they will try to make sense out of what is not sensible. As a result, they are likely to adopt belief systems (world views) that make them feel "in the know" even though their beliefs can be quite wrong. The world view of the traumatized child contains many thinking errors, for example:

- Those who love me will hurt me.
- It is safer to get my needs for closeness met by strangers or those who are not important to me.
- I have to look out for myself, cause nobody else will.
- I have to hurt others before they hurt me.
- I lose myself (I will die) if I become who you want me to be (like you).
- I might as well lie, no one believes me anyway.
- I'm forced to lie when people ask me questions.
- People should stay out of my business.
- If I want something than I should have it.
- If I see something I want I should take it.

- People make me mad.
- When I'm mad I don't care who gets hurt.
- People deserve what they get.
- If I don't get what I want you are to blame.

The cognitive malfunctions of traumatized children manifest in a variety of learning, memory, and intellectual difficulties (e.g., ADHD, auditory processing dysfunction, speech impediments, reading delays, encoding, decoding, and retrieval disturbances). Unfortunately, traumatized children also have been known to fake these difficulties. Sometimes it is nearly impossible to identify what are real problems and what are defense mechanisms, both from a diagnostic perspective as well as from a logic perspective (e.g., It doesn't seem reasonable that a child would fake behaviors that would make her look dumb).

Whether their difficulties are real or fraudulent, it appears many traumatized children find it nearly impossible to keep their rooms, desks, and schoolwork organized. They are often scatterbrained and unable to complete multiple tasks without reminders or other help aides. They often have odd speech patterns, learning lags, and poor cause and effect thinking. Some traumatized children misperceive and misinterpret others' actions as offensive and aggressive and react with paranoia, violence, silliness, chaotic diversions, over cautiousness, or withdrawal (e.g., hiding, silence). In many cases these children are uncoachable because they truly "believe" they are more competent and smarter than adults (especially parents). This fallacious belief in part explains why they are surprised when adults can easily disprove their elaborate lies. These children can be very book smart, but they are not necessarily people or street smart.

Summary

One explanation for cognitive malfunction amongst the traumatized child population is that these children did not master early cognitive stages of development, and did not have enough positive social interactions with more competent partners. Many traumatized children are arrested at the pre-operational stage of cognitive development and have difficulty transitioning into concrete operational thinking because they work hard at avoiding reality. It follows then that many traumatized children will never attain formal operational thinking because they will not be receptive to intellectual and philosophical discussions in which there are no clear-cut answers, and their ways of thinking will be challenged and perhaps proven wrong.

Moral Development

To be moral is to abide by specific codes of conduct prescribed by conventional laws, religious mandates, and/or universal ethics meant to govern all behavior. One is not born with morality, instead it develops over time in the same ways that cognitive and social skills develop, and it is equally vulnerable to environmental conditions. Moral behavior is accompanied by one's understanding of the prescribed codes of conduct and the reasoning one uses to justify the behaviors. According to Kohlberg, understanding and reasoning follow a specific course of development that consists of six steps within three stages.

Stage one: Preconvention - toddlers believe that
    1) might makes right (if you are bigger, you rule),
       and later
    2) you have to look out for yourself first.
Stage two: Conventional - children believe it's
    3) more important to be liked than to do what is
       right, and later
    4) more important to obey the law.
Stage three: Post Conventional, adults believe in
    5) social contracts (all the rules of etiquette and
       vows that formal laws do not cover), and a few
       will attain,
    6) universal principles (e.g., freedom, justice,
       equality for all.)

An example of Preconventional moral ability and reasoning is a child who demands the last scoop of chocolate ice cream because it's her house and her bowls and spoons and so she should get what she wants: step #1 "might makes right." If, instead, she gives her friend the last scoop of chocolate ice cream, because she wants her friend to give her a prized possession, she is demonstrating step #2 "looking out for number one." However, if she gives her friend the last scoop of chocolate ice cream because she wants her friend to like her, even though she knows her mother was saving that scoop, then she is demonstrating step #3. Although the action of giving the scoop of ice cream to her friend is the same, the child's reasoning is quite different and demonstrates different levels of moral ability (the former being lower than the latter).

Randolph (2002) further describes how Kohlberg's stages and steps translate into children's social relationships and behaviors. Between the ages of one to two and a half, children believe it's okay to do whatever you want, but you should avoid misbehaving so that you don't get punished. By age five, children behave because they fear their parents will be angry and will withdraw their love. By age seven, children behave to prove they love their parents. By age nine, children behave because they want other children to like them. By adolescence, children behave because they don't want to hurt others.

An immature moral ability is one of the defining traits of traumatized children. An individual's moral reasoning and ability are most evident when she is confronted with a conflict between two appealing choices (also called a moral dilemma). These choices are usually set within a complex context that goes beyond simple preferences (choosing between vanilla or chocolate ice cream is not a moral dilemma unless you and your best friend both choose the chocolate and there is only one scoop left). In many instances acting morally entails sacrificing some of your needs or wants for another person's needs or wants.

But many traumatized children are often stuck in the preconventional stage of moral development. For these children, choices aren't difficult because they only consider their own wants and needs and do not take other people's views into consideration (Fonagy, 2001); they don't' have moral dilemmas. They are overly invested in winning, often at any cost. They know and can recite the rules but have not internalized them (made them their own), which is why they will often behave properly in the presence of adults and improperly when adults are not present. Plus, breaking the rules is rewarding in and of itself. If they break the rules they win because might makes right.

What's worse, punishment is not an effective deterrent to negative behavior because traumatized children have already been punished in the most egregious manners. Therefore, idle threats and minor consequences are not relevant. There is little that normal, healthy adults can bestow on a traumatized child that would be an effective punishment. Using consequences instead of punishment may be of greater use in inspiring moral behavior, but it is more likely the child will respond to the consequence to avoid being inconvenienced as opposed to having some newly learned understanding or caring for others (see parenting section: difference between punishment and consequences). Perhaps, in time, the use of consequences will help a child develop an internalized moral code that permeates her existence, but that could take years.

Aside from generalized misconduct and selfish choices (often under the guise of having fun), traumatized children with immature moral abilities are often void of spiritual connection. Some relate, instead, to cults or dark magic. Many traumatized children believe God caused their abuse or, at the very least, believe God thinks they deserved to be mistreated. And in all fairness to a child's way of thinking, in what kind of world does God allow little defenseless children to be abused? Unable to turn to God, but still needing to belong, some traumatized children find solace in what is contrary to societal norms -- hence cults and dark magic.

Some traumatized children's low moral ability goes beyond misconduct and selfish or misguided choices -- some become predators. This comes in many shapes and sizes from casual teasing, to relentless bullying, to killing animals and even people. However, for many traumatized children it takes the form of sexual reactivity (in preadolescence) or sexual aggressiveness (in adolescence). All children are highly sexual beings who find great pleasure in touching their own genitals and other areas of their bodies that have high concentrations of nerve cells. Toddlers are very open about this bodily exploration until they realize that others are offended by it. Through social conditioning, the offending child learns to suppress early childhood sexual feelings and behaviors because he desires to fit in, to be accepted, and to please others, which supersedes the desire to pleasure himself. He discovers that the pleasure he receives from social interactions is more satisfying and longer lasting than self-pleasure. Exemptions to this social conditioning include children who are highly anxious and may use masturbation as a form of relief and/or children with semi-constituted or non-constituted attachment.

Children with semi-constituted or non-constituted attachment, who do not seek the joy and comfort of their social worlds, continue to pleasure themselves, and will do so by exploiting others as opposed to joining with others. Satisfaction is found in the ability to offend and the ability to take what is wanted. When there is no reason to sacrifice one's own wants for the needs of others, there is no morality, and no prosocial behavioral code of conduct.

Sexually reactive or aggressive children most likely: 1) were sexually abused themselves, 2) were exposed to prolonged episodes of domestic violence, which may have included sexual assault upon their mothers, 3) observed sexual acts and other sexually explicit material, or 4) all of the above; shockingly, as many as 85% of those children in foster care have experienced some type of sexual abuse. Social learning theory makes it easy to understand why a child who had been sexually abused would then go on to sexually abuse others. Children do what they are taught. However, not all children who suffer early sexual abuse or exposure to domestic violence or sexual acts become sexually reactive or aggressive. And, those who are sexually reactive may never become sexually aggressive (may out grow the desire when they enter puberty).

Unfortunately, there is no way of knowing who will perpetuate the abuse and who will not. Many researchers depend on surveys of risk and protective factors for determining the likelihood of a child becoming a sexual offender. For example, a child who has experienced the above-stated situations is less likely to become a sexual offender if he has an easy temperament, is intelligent, has areas of achievement, and good relationships with parents and peers. A child who has experienced the above stated situations is more likely to become a sexual offender if he has a difficult temperament, low intelligence and academic achievement, poor social skills, disrupted attachments, co morbid conditions (e.g., ADHD, relationship or mood disorders, mental illness), a dysfunctional family structure, and continued exposure to violence (Latham, 1999).

THE PARENT-CHILD RELATIONSHIP

Traumatized children (those children exposed to abuse, neglect, and chaos during early childhood) are different from non-traumatized children. This has been demonstrated in studies of the disrupted attachments of foster and adopted children and the resultant plethora of negative behaviors, attitudes, and beliefs they demonstrate (Bacon & Richardson, 2001; Bolton, 1983; Cline, 1979; Levy and Orlans, 1998; Randolph, 2001; Richters & Volkmar, 1994; Stroufe, 1997). More recently, studies on the effects of trauma on early brain development have made the distinctions between traumatized and non-traumatized children even more clear and disturbing (Fonagy, 1993; Goldberg, Muir & Perry, 1995; Schore 2001; Thompson, 1993). However, one area of study regarding traumatized children has been neglected -- that of their parent-child relationships.

This is an important area of study because child development unfolds within the context of parent-child interactions (Darling, & Steinberg, 1993; Fogel, 1991; Hinde and Stevenson-Hinde, 1987; Maccoby, & Martin, 1983), yet traumatized children often find it effortful, awkward, and frightening to use parent-child relationships as a positive context for development (Fonagy, 1993; Cline, 1979; Levy and Orlans, 1998; Randolph, 2001). In addition, traumatized children's social relatedness problems are often more striking in their parent-child relationships compared to their peer relationships or relationships with other adults (Cline, 1979; Levy and Orlans, 1998; Power & Krause, 1995; Randolph, 2001; Waters, Kondo-Ikemura, Richters, & Posada, 1991).

Furthermore, these negative behaviors and attitudes do not automatically vanish when children are removed from traumatizing environments and placed in healthy, safe environments with surrogate parents. This realization is baffling to professionals and lay people alike because it is counterintuitive to our beliefs about the resiliency of children, the healing power of love, and the protective and nurturing atmospheres of healthy families.

Studying the parent-child relationships of traumatized children is made more difficult because there isn't a framework for studying parent-child relationships in general. In fact, while there is an abundance of research regarding the effects of parenting behavior on child outcomes (for review see: Martin & Martin, ;Maccoby, 1992), there is very little research on parent-child relationships at all (see Cook 1993 for exception).

To create one possible framework, I examined transactional and socio- biological models of development, and the literature on peer relationships and adult relationships. I then created a theory of the structure and function of parent-child relationships based on my examinations, and then applied this theory to parent-child relationships of traumatized children and their surrogate parents. Finally, I developed an alternative/adjunct methodology for studying these relationships and a corresponding intervention for activating the traumatized child's prosocial engagement circuitry.

The Transactional Model of Parent-Child Relationships

There is a question as to whether parental influence determines child outcomes, or whether child characteristics determine parental responses. But this is as tedious a question as the nature-nurture controversy proposed earlier. According to the transactional model of child development the answer is, of course, both: parents effect children and children effect parents.

The parent-child relationship consists of both exogenous factors and endogenous factors. Exogenous factors are personal characteristics or dispositions of the individual that are typical of the individual in all interactions. Endogenous factors are attitudes and interpersonal dispositions of the individuals that are expressed uniquely within the dyad. Therefore, a parent's exogenous factors in combination with a child's exogenous factors equal the endogeny of the dyad with endogeny being the flow between them that is intrinsic to their interactions. What's more, a child's development is intrinsically tied to the parent-child relationship as his individual genotypes are triggered by their endogeny (environment activates a gene which is then filtered through the child's perception of the environment to become an expressed behavior or emotion; Fonagy, 2001).

An infant is born with the propensity for a variety of mental, emotional, and behavioral dispositions, many of which are activated by the environment (e.g., parent-child interactions) within the first three years of life. Likewise, the infant's temperament plus parent-child interactions elicit specific sets of maternal or paternal behaviors that may not have been present prior to that relationship. These can be either good or bad behaviors. For example, an infant who exhibit's attachment needs can evoke feelings of rage and acts of violence in the parent, or unparalleled feelings of love and acts of nurturing. Either response is a result of some exogenous factor of the parent such as unresolved or resolved childhood issues.

The child's personality and dispositional outcomes are determined in part by these parental responses. Also, parental outcomes are affected by child outcomes. For example, infants with difficult temperaments or colic evoke feelings of helplessness in many parents. A parent who cannot cope adequately with these feelings may impose her will on the child and coerce the relationship with fear tactics and love withdrawal. The child may become more dependent, less motivated, and more fearful than if the child had been raised by a mother who learned parenting skills and sought out support to cope with her feelings of helplessness.

Sometimes these situations can spiral out of control as when a parent is so aggravated and overwhelmed by her child's needs and behaviors she feels justified in being abusive; the child is defended against as if she were the cause of the problem. However, given the transactional nature of the parent-child relationship it is not accurate to attribute the cause of abuse and neglect to the child or the parent but rather to their endogeny, although clearly the parent should be held accountable.

A Socio-Biological Perspective

Infants are born with built-in schemas (frameworks) that preserve and organize experiences and help the infant to understand and predict future experiences. Schemas are like index cards in a recipe file box, only instead of labels like desserts, entrees, salads, and soups, etc., the files are labeled events, feelings, language, relationships, surroundings, etc. Each experience is filtered through the infant's senses, perceptions, and his own temperament, and then sorted into the appropriate file. Later experiences flesh out particular files and old and new experiences are reprocessed, cross-referenced and summarized in a variety of ways. For example, frequent and routine experiences are formed into scripts which are then stored as basic facts about a given object, place, or person (Colin, 1996).

Schemas not only provide a framework for preserving and organizing experiences, but also help the infant to unconsciously anticipate that these experiences will and should occur. For example, as discussed earlier, infants are born with certain innate reflexes and behaviors that encourage attachment to a caregiver. Contingent responses from the caregiver are no surprise to the infant (he is not stressed over having his needs met) and these interactions are filed under the relationship schema. A script is soon formed of what the child should continue to expect from that caregiver.

However, when infants experience recurring trauma by a parent, I posit that it is a surprise to the infant. These experiences do not fit with the infant's biological schema of human relationships and what to expect in the caregiver-infant relationship (though I know of no research to support this notion). As such, I further posit that the infant may file these experiences under the threats-to-survival schema and may create a script in which he expects parents indirectly, and sometimes directly, to try to kill him (whether it is physically, emotionally, and/or spiritually).

From a socio-biological perspective, parents abusing and neglecting infants and children is antithetical to human existence; the infant has no innate schema in which to place such experiences. This may have profound implications for later development as the child attempts to assimilate the parental death wish schema into other relationship schemas. For example, the child might adapt a world view and an array of behaviors that are counterproductive to family life because he believes those that are close to you will try to kill you. Alternatively, the child may internalize a profound sense of not belonging, which may make it impossible for him to feel comfortable in relationships and to find life meaningful.

For example, a forty-five year old man who committed suicide had talked about it for years prior to the event. He had been to therapists and although medication was prescribed he only took it sporadically. From the outside he appeared quite successful and was well liked and admired by friends and coworkers. His children loved and adored him but he often said he could not feel it nor could he sustain the feeling of being loved for any length of time. On several occasions during their twelve year marriage he told his wife that he had a distinct sense that he was not supposed to be here (alive). He was an abused and neglected child. And from a sociobiological perspective one could presume that these early experiences of trauma made suicide a viable option to solving normal problems of daily living and relationship management. He wasn't supposed to be alive anyway!

Relationship Literature

According to Webster's dictionary, a relationship is the quality or state of being connected. To say that people are in a relationship usually means that they are not only connected by blood, marriage, or circumstance, but are involved in a series of interactions over time. However, not all relationships are alike. They vary in structure (inherent systematic organization of parts that is mostly unchangeable), and in function (specialized actions of the parts that are somewhat variable and help sustain the structure). When considering the structure and function of relationships, the parent-child relationship differs from peer relationships (both child to child and adult to adult) in at least five ways.

Structure of Parent-Child Relationships
Involuntary Membership

Peer relationships are easily and voluntarily joined into by people who share qualities or interests. But children and parents do not have the luxury of choosing each other based on some commonality. They are thrust together by circumstance and are expected to remain together. This may appear to be true of children in a classroom setting as well. However, there is choice in this setting because there are so many children in one class, and as such, children tend to voluntarily join into smaller groups within the larger group. Plus, group members sometimes come and go, and a different adult is present each year. A parent-child relationship on the other hand, is the equivalent of an arranged marriage, only permanent.

Permanence

As mentioned above peer relationships can be joined into quite easily. And conversely, they can be dissolved quite easily. When the needs of at least one member of the couple or group are not being met the results are fatal to the relationship and the member leaves or the group disbands or "exits" the relationship. Not so in parent-child relationships. Berscheid, E., Snyder, M., Omoto, A.M. (1989) who devised a Relationship Closeness Inventory (RCI) found that dissolution of a relationship is obvious in romantic relationships, is a hardly noticeable withering process in platonic relationships, and virtually non-existent in most family relationships. Children and parents can not choose which families they would like to be a member of, nor can they opt out of a family relationship; dissolution of the parent-child relationship is usually not a viable option, even when individual needs are not being satisfied (exceptions include death, divorce, children running away from home, or interventions by social service agencies that remove children from their homes).

Dependency

Peers are drawn together based on proximity first and commonalities second, and often find some need satisfaction in their interactions (or they would probably "exit" the relationship). But in parent-child relationships, children rely heavily on parents for almost all of their physical and emotional needs satisfaction. And, parents rely heavily on children for many of their emotional needs satisfaction. This in part explains why dissolution of peer relationships is not fatal to the individual members (they often move on to other peer or group memberships with little to no consequence). Yet, should dissolution occur in parent-child relationships the members are often devastated and the return to homeostasis can be a long and painful process.

Long-Term Physical Proximity

Physical proximity is not necessary to maintain voluntary groups or sustain member survival. In addition, because time spent together in voluntary groups is limited, avoidance of unpleasant situations or individuals is possible. However, in parent-child relationships long-term physical proximity is not only obligatory to maintain the group but is vital for the survival of younger members. And because of this structure, avoiding unpleasantness is rarely possible.

Inequality of Power

Peer relationships are characterized by equality and cooperation (Brody & Shaffer, 1982; Eisenberg, & Mussen,1989; Nucci, Killen, & Smetna, 1996; Youniss,1980). But, parent-child relationships are typically characterized by a major inequality of power (Amato, 1990; Crockenberg, Jackson, & Langrock, 1996; Walker & Taylor, 1991; Youniss, 1980). Walker and Taylor (1991) point out that power differences between parents and children are so obvious and inescapable that equality is not possible; that is, the power difference is an ever-present fact of the relationship, and both parent and child are aware of this fact on some level. The size difference alone between parents and children connotes a power differential, which does not exist in peer relationships; many young children are afraid of adults just because adults are bigger than they are.

This atypical structure (i.e., involuntary membership, permanence, dependency, physical proximity, and inequality,) underlying all parent-child relationships, whether healthy or not, appears uncomfortable and untenable to say the least and should predict relationship failure. After all, would a child enter into a relationship that was forced on him and that he couldn't just walk away from; a relationship in which he was completely dependent on "the other" for his very survival and could not avoid "the other" when she acted badly or displayed some undesirable trait; a relationship in which "the other" had most of the power and responsibility? And would an adult enter into a relationship that was forced on her and that she couldn't just walk away from; a relationship in which "the other" was completely dependent on her for his very survival and she could not avoid "the other" when he acted badly or displayed some undesirable trait; a relationship in which she had most of the power but also most of the responsibility?

Surprisingly, the answer to these questions seems to be a resounding "Yes;" most people do want to be in a parent-child relationship and quite often these relationships do not fail and are satisfying to both members. Why? In addition to biological mechanisms that serve to maintain the relationship, I propose that healthy families adopt, often unknowingly but sometimes deliberately, a unique functionality that ensures success and satisfaction within the imposed structure. And it is the function as opposed to the structure that makes parent-child relationships so desirable.

Function of Parent-Child Relationships
Falling in Love and Commitment
To facilitate the structure of involuntary membership, parents and children fall in love with each other through the attachment process and stay committed to one another, often throughout the life span.

Specialness in Belonging
To facilitate the structure of permanence, parents and children create specialness in their belonging to each other through shared rituals, story telling of family history, photos and videos of time spent together, and discovery and nurturing of shared interests.

Predictability and Stability

To facilitate the structure of dependency parents and children strive for predictability and stability in their relationship. Predictability and stability create the "illusion" of independence. That is, routines and clear expectations remove capriciousness from the equation, which increases opportunities for acting independently and lessens the occurrence of "learned helplessness" (reaction to prolonged exposure to unpredictable and uncontrollable circumstances).

Stress Reducing Activities

To facilitate the structure of long-term physical proximity parents and children create outlets and coping mechanisms to relieve the stress associated with inherent togetherness and unavoidable unpleasantness.

Reciprocity

To facilitate the structure of inequality, parents and children operate from a foundation of reciprocity. All human relationships, including parent-child relationships entail some form of reciprocity, such as correspondent reciprocity (conformity, to be similar or equal). However, parent-child relationships operate more often from a foundation of complementary reciprocity (acts/parts that complete each other and create a whole). Piaget explained this as a principle in which responses are the product of duration and intensity of stimulation. Therefore, a weak stimulus of infinite duration may equal a brief stimulus of higher intensity. The responses are complementary but not equal.

How It All Works (and doesn't work)

In addition to falling in love through the attachment process (explained in the previous section), parents and children experience strong bonds of commitment to, and investment in, each other. When most parents bring children into the world, it is with the profound understanding that they are responsible for raising them until they are at least eighteen, and will be involved with them beyond childhood. The parents' biological urge to protect, nurture, and guide their children insures this commitment, as does societal norms that challenge and scorn those who do not fulfill their duties as parents. Parental commitment is further strengthened by parents' insatiable curiosity in observing their children's growth to adulthood, and gratification in their children's accomplishments. As children grow, and become more independent and accomplished, the better parents feel about the years of time, money, and energy they invested in their children.

Children, on the other hand, feel strong bonds of commitment, and investment because they recognize their limitations in satisfying their own needs and wants (e.g., safety, security, belonging, food, shelter, companionship, warmth, tactile stimulation). Throughout family life, children rely on their parents for need and want satisfaction to some degree (i.e., all in infancy, most in childhood, some in adolescence, and fewer in early adulthood). But need and want satisfaction is not a forgone conclusion (even though the tacit assumption is that children's needs will be met unconditionally). For their needs and wants to be met children must "buy-in" or commit to the criteria for family membership.

"Buy-in" entails falling in love with parents, accepting the hierarchical family structure, and giving up tyrannical needs for power and control. On-going attachment behaviors resulting in positive child outcomes reinforce the child's "buy-in;" a securely attached child tends to be more compliant with parental directives and as a result tends to benefit more from the reciprocal nature of the relationship than a child who is not securely attached and does not "buy-in." Those children who don't "buy-in," (i.e., don't fall in love with their parents, don't accept parental authority and don't give up control) will not feel accepted, safe and protected, and will lose out on fun, positive interactions (no one wants to play with a controlling, unresponsive child).

Understandably, children feel vulnerable when they "buy-in" because they are dependent on adults for need satisfaction, and feeling vulnerable is often accompanied by some anxiety. However, that anxiety is usually assuaged when the child's needs are consistently and adequately met by the adult. However, if adults are not dependable, the child's anxiety increases. For example, when a child's defensives are exhausted, the child becomes distressed and will look to parents for guidance. However, if parents respond with maturity demands on the child such as telling the child to take care of it herself, or asking the child to take care of the parent instead, or if parents are unavailable altogether, the child's needs may not be met and her anxiety level will increase significantly.

A child's anxiety level will also increase if she perceives the parent to be the cause of her distress. For example, when my daughter was four years old I once scolded her for breaking something. She began to cry and then hugged me around the legs saying, "You hurt my feelings." I praised her for having hurt feelings and told her that's exactly how she should feel when she has done something wrong (even though she misinterpreted why she had hurt feelings in the first place). In this example, my child's bad behavior was actually the direct cause of her distress and my actions were secondary and in response to her behavior. Interestingly, a well attached child will seek out comfort and absolution from the very parent who has just disciplined her; this is a sign of secure attachment.

In the case of the traumatized child, however, it truly is the parent's actions that are causing the distress. The child's investment in her parent fails to produce gratification over and over again, and the child faces the dilemma of seeking guidance and comfort from the very person who is hurting her. In response, the child's bonds of commitment wane, and her investment in her own need satisfaction increases while investment in her parent's need satisfaction decreases. That is, she stops caring about pleasing her parent and seeks alternative ways of pleasing herself and relieving anxiety (the child is still bonded to the parent but she is no longer committed to the relationship).

The anxiety created from unmet need satisfaction and lack of commitment to a relationship far surpasses that created from dependency on responsive adults to satisfy needs. Traumatized children channel their anxiety into aggression, withdrawal, defensiveness, or a facade of friendliness. To insure need satisfaction and a sense of security, they commit to new goals: to protect, maintain, and control their own environment. If they removed from a traumatizing home life, and relocated into a new environment, their goals are put into action with the new family by creating a false reality in which they provide for their own safety, security, food, shelter, companionship, warmth, and tactile stimulation.

One parent I interviewed referred to this as "sneaky self-sufficiency." He said his foster child makes announcements, or thinks out loud saying something like "I'm hungry," or "I'm cold." As a good, attentive parent he immediately provides food or a sweater for the child, realizing later that the child got his needs met without having asked anyone for anything. This father's child was trying to recreate the very earliest stages of infant perceptions, when he believed others to be an extension of him as opposed to separate human beings. And, he was trying to get his needs met without committing to the relationship.

Parental responsiveness to infant announcements (e.g., crying, restlessness) reinforces the perception that the infant is completely efficacious in satisfying his own needs; the parent provides what is needed at the right time. Because the infant cannot yet distinguish between objective and subjective reality, he believes he created what he needed. Eventually the child's subjective reality becomes disillusioned by objective reality -- his parents are separate human beings from him and he is not in control of them, but rather the other way around. He then justly credits his parents for their contributions to his needs satisfaction. As the child grows, his parents stress this natural structure by expecting him to ask for what he wants (e.g., "Use your words.") and to use manners while doing so (e.g., "Say, please and thank you."). And, the child is insured satisfaction and a sense of security by doing so.

But traumatized children must make a conscious effort to "buy-in" to this natural relationship structure and conduct the functions that make the structure work. Those that won't or can't make the effort do not fall in love with the new parents, concede to the hierarchical family structure, or give up their tyrannical need for power and control. Their continued belief that gratification comes only from the self creates pseudo-independence and fosters feelings of superiority and megalomania actions (e.g., presumed entitlement, false pride, exaggeration of abilities, self-stimulation). These children have no need to comply with parental directives and parental expectations of reciprocity because they have no use for parents. As a result, the bonds of commitment never form.

When successful falling in love and commitment to one another occurs, parents and children find many interesting ways of enhancing their relationship and making it more special (something worth belonging to for the rest of your life). Daily rituals (e.g., meal times, bed time routines), aside from creating stability, give all family members something enjoyable to look forward to in the short term. Preparing for and participating in recurring yearly celebrations both secular (birthdays, anniversaries, vacations) and non-secular (religious holidays) leads to anticipation of good things to come over the long term. These events breed a sense of normalcy and instill hope that life will continue and can still be good even when bad things happen.

Visits from grandparents and extended family bring an additional sense of belonging to something larger than oneself. During these visits, members share memories of their collective histories, often commenting on who looks and acts like whom and who was named after which long lost relative. They listen with great interest to the younger members and sometimes join in their activities, creating new memories and new family stories. When most of the sharing is of a positive nature all family members gain a sense that they are a part of something positive, something that lasts, something to be proud of, and something that tells them "I'm supposed to be here."

Many surrogate parents of traumatized children report that their children work hard at destroying these special events; that many of these children can not even enjoy their own birthdays. Many traumatized children missed out on the very events that serve to strengthen familial bonds and make "permanence" not only more tenable but actually desirable. As a result they never became accustomed to that level of intimacy and sharing. And for some, even if these events did occur, having never experienced successful falling in love, and feeling no sense of commitment to others, the events did not ring true, or could not generate a sense of a positive shared history. These events, particularly if they are somewhat out of context with the day to day living of a chaotic or abusive household, may actually lead to more family instability.

According to Webster's Dictionary, something is stable if it is firm and steady, not easily thrown off balance, not likely to break down, give way, or change, is lasting and enduring, and able to return to its original form should it be disturbed (resilient). Stability is an important function of the parent-child relationship, and families in general, because one can not be safely dependent if the environment is easily thrown off balance and is unpredictable. Plus, optimal human development is dependent on a return to homeostasis.

Society imposes certain expectations on the family unit that encourages stability, which enhances optimal development and survival of the species (e.g., marry, stay married, bear children when the marriage proves robust, and care for your children until the legal age of eighteen).

So too do parents impose certain expectations on their families that encourages stability, which assists the smooth running of the family, enhances child resiliency, and fosters the long term goal of interdependence. Parental expectations of a hierarchy of roles, and explicit rules and consequences, and routines and schedules eventually allow children to perform many acts without having to be told what to do, when to do it, and how to do it. The child's reliance on clear and consistent parental expectations increases his capacity to be independent (ergo dependency leads to independence).

Parents who lack these expectations or the skills to enforce them have children who are overwhelmed with worries of uncertainty because there is no logical cause and effect between their actions and their parents' responses. These children do not trust their parents and lose confidence in their parents' abilities to keep them safe and satisfied; these children can not be safely dependent. In addition, when uncertainty is present and predictability is absent "learned helplessness" can occur. An individual exhibiting learned helplessness believes he no longer has any control over his environment because nothing he does diminishes or removes the negative situation. Many traumatized children have "learned helplessness" and some lose the incentive to pursue goals and give up trying all together.

Interfamily attachment, commitment, and belonging should guarantee long-term cohesiveness and stability of the family unit. However, this is not always the case. Families experience common (e.g., divorce) and extraordinary (e.g., 9/11) events that compromise the family structure and, as a result, nullify the guarantee. The loss of a parent, for example, can be devastating to the family financially and emotionally, and changes the organization as a whole. Loss of a parent is particularly difficult for children because their coping mechanisms, identities, and sense of independence are not fully developed yet.

However, a child who once knew stability and now must face reorganization due to the loss of a parent is likely to have a good enough emotional foundation plus additional familial support to help him cope with the crisis (resiliency). Still, even the most emotionally healthy child may struggle with this change. A traumatized child who never knew stability because interfamily emotional bonds were compromised or annihilated by the emotional inaccessibility of the parent and the parent's anti-family behaviors, is likely to fare much worse because he lacks a good enough emotional foundation and family support to cope with the loss. Should the child be removed from his home, as in social service interventions, he will lose all members of his family. And, he will be placed into a family structure in which dependency is presumed and stability provided. This may be as much of a shock to the child as the loss of his family.

The stronger the attachments are to the birth family, the more devastating the emotional trauma of losing them is to the child. On the other hand, strong attachments and commitments to others also increase the likelihood that the child will successfully transition into a new family, eventually. If these children are frequently moved, however, they may begin to resemble children with weak attachments to others and strong commitments to self. The weaker the attachment and commitments are to the birth family or a foster family at the time of removal, the more confident the child will be in her negative assessments of the world (e.g., you can't depend on anyone, stability is not possible, adults say one thing and do another, nobody who loves you sticks around). As a result the child's anti-social/ family behaviors may increase (e.g., overly developed defense mechanisms, impaired learning, hyper vigilance, pseudo-independence, inauthenticity) when she attempts to live within a structure she believes can and will change at any moment. This belief system adds stress to a structure that is already inherently stressful due to physical proximity.

It is a paradox that physical proximity in healthy parent-child relationships is inherently protective and satisfying, but at the same time may be inherently stressful and aggravating. For example, physical proximity allows us countless opportunities for physical contact. (e.g., grabbing a hug from our loved one when ever we feel like it). This is lovely if both people are in the mood. However, should one or the other not be in the mood this action can be quite stressful -- a situation in which both parents and children sometimes find themselves. In other words, while physical proximity may encourage the use of actions meant to increase comfort and safety, it may also result in feeling smothered and invaded. In addition, all people have strengths and weaknesses, good parts and not so good parts. The fact that family members are expected to live together in close physical proximity allows us to enjoy the good parts of each other quite often, but makes it nearly impossible to avoid the not so good parts. This causes stress for the whole family.

Children are particularly susceptible to these stressful feelings because their free movement is restricted, their goals often come second to the goals of their parents, privacy is not always available, parents mistakenly believe their children are unaware of their bad parts or will not remember the display of negative behaviors, and children have fewer resources to satisfy their needs and do not have the option to leave their family situations to get their needs met elsewhere (until late into adolescence). One way parents help to relieve this inherent relationship stress, and reduce their children's sense of dependency is by sharing power and control with their children while not abdicating the very authority that substantiates stability (see authoritative parenting style).

Unfortunately, ineffective parents are unskilled in recognizing their children's stress and in sharing power and control. These parents either give away their power and control by spoiling their children (e.g., giving unearned toys and privileges, and having low expectations of responsibility fulfillment) or greedily hold on to their power and control by dictating their children's feelings and behaviors. As a result these children never learn to earn, choose, give, or shift from a state of dependency to interdependency.

A second strategy families implement to relieve the tensions associated with physical proximity is fun. Laughter and play are great stress relievers. Healthy families incorporate a variety of individual and family fun activities and often know how to find humor in many of the frustrations of day to day living. Ineffective parents, however often invest in their own fun but not in creating safe fun for their children. They may abandon their children for periods of time or may use drugs and alcohol to relieve the stress associated with family responsibilities and the onerous task of raising children. In this way they substitute one dependency for another. They often don't know how to have fun with their children in ways that are appropriate for children. I know of several mothers who took their children on "family vacations" with the mothers' adult "friends." The children shared hotel rooms with these friends and were exposed to drugs and sexual activity. These parents often adultify their children believing that it's only fair that the child receive the same experiences and privileges as the parent.

What these families most lack is an understanding of the function of complementary reciprocity. Reciprocity begins with the coordination of actions between parent and infant. Coordination, or lack of coordination, determines how each person will fare individually and in the relationship, both physically and emotionally. Although parents and infants are not equals, their coordinated actions can result in outcomes of equal value. For example, when the baby cries, the parents pick up the baby, feed the baby, change the baby, etc. When the baby coos, the parents coo back, play with the baby, give the baby a toy, etc. The baby, in essence, has evoked the parents to take action and the parents have acted in contingently responsive ways. Of course, the parents are doing most of the work here, but the parents and the child are satisfied with their perspective, but different, outcomes.

The outcomes for the baby include valid and reliable knowledge of a safe and predictable environment over which she has some control, inhibition of learned helplessness (Lewis & Sullivan, 1994), trust in the parents' abilities to satisfy her needs, and a working model for future communication skills (Bretherton, 1992). The outcomes for the parents include a sense of trust and competency in their abilities to satisfy their infant's needs (the infant's trust cycle corresponds with the parent's trust cycle), and joy in the interaction.

Hence, parents and infants coordinating their actions and acting in-kind results in a reciprocal relationship; their outcomes are not identical but they may be of equal value and importance to the respective members of the dyad. This reciprocal foundation is played out throughout childhood as family members prompt and reinforce desirable behaviors in each other and, as a result, feel good about themselves and the people they live with.

However, as explained earlier in the section on attachment, traumatized children's parent-child interactions sometimes lack coordination, and, therefore, neither fare well individually or in the relationship. Trust cycles are not satisfied, needs are not met, desirable behaviors are not prompted, and neither feels good about himself or herself or the relationship. Rather than learning how to reciprocate, children who missed out on coordinated parent-child interactions learn how to defend. Having never learned how to respond to valid and reliable sources of love and nurturing, when they are presented with it at a later date, they tend to respond with what they initially received -- criticism, disregard, fear, and anger. Also, because early infant-parent reciprocal interactions help to create a working model for children's communication skills, children who did not experience these interactions often communicate like television sets -- they spew information at you, do not listen for responses to their questions, and do not engage in dialogue.

What's more, children who are treated like equals by their parents and exposed to too much, too soon are likely to expect equal treatment and equal outcomes. No longer are they satisfied with what children should receive in the relationship, they want what the parent receives. This now resembles a peer relationship in which competition for resources is a common practice and in which children lose the opportunity and benefits of being taught by an older wiser guide.

Recap: Healthy Parent-Child Relationships

Falling in Love and Commitment
- Adults are biologically programmed to feel compassionate and warm towards infants.
- Parents feel innate sense and societal expectation of responsibility to raise their own children and provide for all of their children's needs.
- Parents have on-going curiosity and pride in their children's development and outcomes.
- Infants are biologically programmed to seek out the human face, and they have fixed reflex patterns that evoke attachment behaviors in adults.
- Children feel a sense of obligation and loyalty to their parents when parents satisfy children's needs. As a result children want to please their parents.

Specialness and Belonging
- Parents create family routines, rituals, and celebrations, in which children play an important role and have clear identities.
- Parents talk positively about family histories and children's contributions to the family, and share activities that create new memories.
- Children participate in these events with joy, hope, and anticipation.
- Children, through their own activities, add new family stories.

Predictability and Stability
- Parents impose a hierarchy of roles, rules and consequences, routines and schedules, predictability and consistency, and a logical system of responsibilities and privileges.
- Children abide by parental directives and internalize self-control.

Stress Reducing Activities
- Parents implement fun (for themselves and their children), are affectionate, provide appropriate choices (share power), shelter children from adult matters, and allow for privacy.
- Children play, and seek out affection and comfort from their parents even if they believe parents are the cause of their distress.

Complementary Reciprocity
- Starting in infancy, coordination of actions between parent and child results not in equal behaviors or outcomes, but in outcomes that are of equal value to each.
- Family members prompt and reinforce desirable behaviors in each other throughout childhood and the duration of the relationship.

Recap: Unhealthy Parent-Child Relationships

Superficial Love and Commitment to Self
- Child and Parental love is based on bonding event but not on attachment behaviors.
- Parents shun responsibilities and lack attunement skills. Place their needs satisfaction before their

children's needs satisfaction.
- Children invest in their own need satisfaction and pleasing themselves.
- Children create fantasy worlds and channel anxiety into negative (anti-family) behaviors.

Isolation
- Parents fail to implement consistent rituals, routines, and celebrations, and spend little time with children.
- Parents have few positive family history stories, or the stories do not match reality.
- Children are unattached to a world that is greater than themselves.
- Children create a sense of identity from superficial or negative activities.

Unpredictability and Instability
- Parents are unreliable and there are few or logical rules and consequences, or routines and schedules.
- Roles are confused or reversed.; parent depends on child for care-giving.
- Children use/manipulate others to get what they want.
- Children's behaviors and attitudes grow increasingly unstable and aggressive to mimic their environments.

Added Stress with No Relief
- Parents do not create logical cause and effect patterns between the child's needs and actions and their responses (unpredictability).
- Parents have poor boundaries with child

- Parents fail to protect and buffer their children from adult matters (chaotic or overtly sexual life style).
- Parents entertain themselves but provide few safe, fun outlets for children.
- Children make their own fun, often in destructive ways.
- As the child's needs go unmet, the child becomes more and more needy, pushes parental buttons, causes problems at school, etc.

Foundation of Competition
- Starting in infancy, lack of coordination of actions between parent and child results in need for equal outcomes (corresponding reciprocity), not equal value of outcomes (complementary reciprocity).
- Family members compete for basic need satisfaction and prized outcomes (stuff).
- Family members prompt and reinforce negative behaviors in each other throughout childhood and the duration of the relationship.

Benefits of a Parent-Child Relationship Perspective:

In conjunction with what is now known about early brain development, a parent-child relationship perspective expands our understanding of why shifting the traumatized child's environment does not always result in desired outcomes. When traumatized children are placed in surrogate families they enter with the knowledge of the objectionable structure but not of the desirable, practical, and effective function of the relationship. These experiences are now in effect hard-wired in the child's brain and the expectation that new positive experiences will be embraced and assimilated by the child simplifies and discounts the role of early parent-child interactions, and perception and interpretation in human thinking and behavior.

These expectations also set the stage for failure and disappointment, both for the child and the surrogate parents. Parents who foster or adopt a traumatized child often do so under the assumption that the child is interested and willing to be in a parent-child relationship. It seems natural and automatic to make this assumption, particularly when the structure is in place (i.e., you place a younger human being with an older human being, they did not choose each other but they live in the same house together, the younger human being is dependent on the older human being, and the older human being tells the younger human being what and how to do things.)

However, the surrogate parents also expect reciprocity, positive engagement, appreciation, respect, and cooperation from these children. At the same time the children expect chaos, competition, freedom, self-reliance and personal satisfaction of all wants. When neither the parents nor the children's expectations are met, both are often sorely disappointed and frustrated. What is discovered is that this is not a parent-child relationship at all, but an arranged marriage of sorts, in which both members find themselves trapped. This discovery should inform both parenting practices and therapeutic interventions, which will be explored in the following two sections.

Summary

The perspective provided by The Transactional Model suggests that parents and children contribute to each other's outcomes, both individually and in the relationship, by how they interpret and respond to each other's attitudes and behaviors. Stressors experienced by either the child or the parent can result in the manifestation of behaviors previously not present and possibly only present within the endogeny of their relationship.

A socio-biological perspective provides a dramatic interpretation of the damage trauma inflicts on the infant/child psyche. From these two models in combination with the relationship literature, a structure and function of parent-child relationships emerges. Unfortunately, traumatized children have experience with the somewhat objectionable structure of parent-child relationships, but rarely experience a healthy functioning of this relationship.

TRAUMATIZED CHILDREN'S BEHAVIORAL MANIFESTATIONS

Parent Reports of Negative Behaviors

The negative behaviors of traumatized children reported by their foster/adoptive parents are strikingly similar and appear to fall into one of three categories: Immoral, Destructive, and Annoying. Luckily, most of these behaviors fall into the annoying category. As I delineate these behaviors, some of you may say to yourselves "All children do that." This is true, all children display one or more of these behaviors, attitudes, beliefs at some time or another. As a matter of fact, all of them can be considered normal if they occur during the first five years of life. However, traumatized children display more than their fair share of these behaviors, attitudes, and beliefs with predictable regularity throughout their childhood. The duration, frequency, intensity, and sheer multitude of these behaviors, attitudes, and beliefs far surpass those of "non-traumatized" children. Furthermore, these behaviors are highly resistant to any intervention, unlike children with discipline problems (see discipline vs. behavior problems).

The following is by no means an exhaustive list. Traumatized children exhibit many other disconcerting behaviors, some of which have been discussed in other sections of this book. (e.g., not learning from past mistakes, not taking responsibility for their actions, etc.) The display of any one of these behaviors does not suggest a disturbance in the child. However, the display of a number of these behaviors after the age of five, that are resistant to change through appropriate consequences, is a red flag.

Immoral Behaviors

Sexual behavior: As mentioned earlier sexual acting out is common among traumatized children. Statistically speaking, eighty five percent of children who have been in three or more placements (either voluntary or involuntary) will be or have been sexually abused. Statistics of how many of these children will go on to sexually abuse others vary widely as do treatment modalities. Sexually acting out consists of flirting behaviors (e.g., batting eyes, rubbing up against each other, high sweet voices, whispering, holding hands, silliness, dumbing down, feigned interest in other's activities) and more aggressive behaviors (e.g., grabbing each other's genitals, pulling pants down, fondling, and rape). Other sexual activities include obsessive masturbation, masturbation with objects, imitation of sexual intercourse, imitating sexual behavior with dolls, sexual sounds, open-mouth kissing, undressing other people, and asking to watch sexually explicit movies (Latham, 1999).

Stealing is a common behavior of traumatized children. Many traumatized children steal and horde food, which is certainly understandable. What is more concerning, however, are the children who steal from family, friends and neighbors and who steal items they have absolutely no use for. Traumatized children steal for a variety of reasons: (1) it's a response to a paratactic distortion (the child truly believes he needs to steal to survive), (2) the stolen object represents the birth parent over whom the child believes he has rights, (3) it's a conditioned behavior taught by caregivers, (4) disregard for societal norms (low moral reasoning), (5) a response to having been taken away from a caregiver (pay back), and/or (6) self-stimulation (to raise stress hormones or stress-reducing hormones).

Lying: Traumatized children exhibit the whole gamut of lying behavior: white lies (to save someone's feelings), developmental lies (don't know the difference between fantasy and truth), and anti-social lies (to save themselves from getting into trouble, to get what they want, or to take advantage of someone). What is most disturbing for parents however, is "crazy" lying in which the child (1) wants to appear "in the know" and will continue to deny facts even in the face of overwhelming evidence, (2) lies just to disagree and the consequence is not connected to any apparent benefit to the child, or (3) lies to get caught so that you will know how clever she is. Crazy lying results in one of two things: either the parent feels crazy or the child looks crazy. Experienced parents know it is the latter and not the former.

There is another type of lying prevalent in traumatized children that I call "shame reduction" lying. Some traumatized children believe they are perfect and smarter than everyone else (it is a component of their "independence" fantasy). Confrontation with the fact that they are not perfect or smarter is intolerable and fills them with overwhelming feelings of shame. Therefore, they will lie if telling the truth would reveal their imperfections.

Hurting/controlling others and animals can be obvious or not, and can be physical, sexual, or emotional. Obvious hurting and controlling is fairly easy to deal with, but many traumatized children are amazingly underhanded in their abuse of others. They will act hyper to get other children wound up, have lots of accidents during which other children get hurt, hide other children's toys, manipulate/coerce other children into giving them stuff, and physically threaten other children who don't do things their way. Many parents of traumatized children will report that their child loves the family dog, but fail to recognize how the child is controlling the animal by smothering it, holding it against its will, or crushing or squeezing it all in the name of playing.

Abusing Parents is a common practice of some traumatized children. It is hard to imagine that children can be abusers. However, a clear comparison can be made when you place the traumatized child's abusing behaviors side by side with that of perpetrators of domestic violence.

Adult Perpetrator

What is your relationship like?

Do you feel that something is wrong with your relationship, but you don't know how to describe it?

Do you feel that your partner controls your life?

Do you feel that your partner does not value your thoughts or feelings?

Will your partner do anything to win an argument, such as put you down, threaten or intimidate you?

Does your partner get angry and jealous if you talk to someone else?

Do you feel that you cannot do anything right in your partner's eyes?

Does your partner demand to know where you are and what you are doing at all times?

Does your partner call you names?

Are you prevented from going to work or school?

Abusive Child

What is your relationship like?

Do you feel that something is wrong with your relationship, but you don't know how to describe it?

Do you feel that your child controls your life?

Do you feel that your child does not value your thoughts or feelings?

Will your child do anything to win an argument, such as put you down, threaten or intimidate you?

Does your child get angry and jealous if you talk to someone else?

Do you feel that you cannot do anything right in your child's eyes?

Does your child demand to know where you are and what you are doing at all times?

Does your child call you names?

Does your child restrict your activities because no one else can or will care for him/her?

Does your child blame you for everything that goes wrong?

Adult Perpetrator

Abusive Behavior

Stalking / Harassing Behavior - following; turning up at workplace or house; parking outside; repeated phone calls or mail to victim and/or family, friends, colleagues.

Threats & Intimidation - threatening to harm you, self or others (children, family, friends, pets); banging on the house windows or doors; threatening to make reports to authorities that jeopardize child custody.

Economic Abuse - controlling or stealing money; fostering dependency; making financial decisions without asking or telling partner.

Sexual Abuse/Harassment - forcing sex or specific acts, pressuring into unwanted sexual behavior, criticizing performance.

Property Destruction - destroying mementos, breaking furniture or windows, throwing or smashing objects, trashing clothes or other possessions.

Abusive Child

Abusive Behavior

Stalking / Harassing Behavior – following you around the house, attacking you with questions, non-stop begging or pleading, sneaking around the house.

Threats & Intimidation - threatening to harm you, self or others (children, family, friends, pets); threatening to make false reports to authorities about being abused.

Economic Abuse - stealing money from you

Sexual Abuse/Harassment – acts sexually provocative towards you, too much or inappropriate touching or physical contact, becomes angry when sexual behavior is not reciprocated.

Property Destruction - destroying mementos, breaking furniture or windows, throwing or smashing objects, trashing clothes or other possessions.

Adult Perpetrator

How are you affected?

Are you unable or afraid to make decisions for yourself?

Do you do anything you can to please your partner or not upset him/her?

Do you make excuses for your partner's behavior?

Are you forgetful, confused or unable to concentrate?

Have you noticed changes in your eating, sleeping, alcohol or drug use?

Have you lost interest or energy to do the things you used to?

Do you feel sick, anxious, tired or depressed a lot of the time?

Have you lost contact with your friends, family or neighbors?

Have you lost self-confidence?

Abusive Child

How are you affected?

Are you feeling confused and disoriented as to how to parent your child?

Do you do anything you can to please your child or not upset him/her?

Do you make excuses for your child's behavior?

Are you forgetful, confused or unable to concentrate?

Have you noticed changes in your eating, sleeping, alcohol or drug use?

Have you lost interest or energy to do the things you used to?

Do you feel sick, anxious, tired or depressed a lot of the time?

Have you lost contact with your friends, family or neighbors?

Have you lost self-confidence?

Adult Perpetrator

What can you do about it?

Recognize that emotional abuse is as bad or worse than physical abuse.

Take your own safety and the safety of your children seriously.

Know that you are not to blame for your partner's abusive behavior.

Find people to talk to that can support you.

Do not give up if community professionals are not helpful. Keep looking for someone that will listen to you and take emotional abuse seriously.

Recognize that you have the right to make your own decisions, in your own time, and that dealing with any form of abuse may take time.

Trust yourself and your own experiences. Believe in your own strengths. Remember that you are your own best source of knowledge and strength.

Abusing Child

What can you do about it?

Recognize that emotional abuse is as bad or worse than physical abuse.

Take your own safety and the safety of your children seriously.

Know that you are not to blame for your child's abusive behavior.

Find people to talk to that can support you.

Do not give up if community professionals are not helpful. Keep looking for someone that will listen to you and take emotional abuse seriously.

Recognize that you have the right to make your own

decisions, in your own time, and that dealing with any form of abuse may take time.

Trust yourself and your own experiences. Believe in your own strengths. Remember that you are your own best source of knowledge and strength.

Destructive Behaviors

Fire setting: There are two basic types of fire-setting: (1) contained - child sets a fire in a small waste can or in the middle of a tile floor in a bathroom, (2) non-contained - child sets fire to bedding, carpet, curtains, or the perimeter of the house. Contained fire-setting often signifies a cry for attention and help. Sometimes, contained fires become out of control and cause much damage, but that was probably not the child's intent. Non-contained fires are most often set with destruction in mind. These children either want to cause damage, just because they can, or they believe, quite mistakenly, that if they burn down their foster/adoptive homes and their foster/adoptive parents, they will be returned to their birth mothers. As you can imagine, the character of the latter is much more suspect than that of the former, and these children should probably not reside in a family setting until this behavior is extinguished (excuse the pun).

Bed-wetting: Bed-wetting is one of those behaviors that can still be considered normal after the age of five, particularly at night and if the child is male. Many parents of bed-wetters take their children to the doctor to rule out any medical conditions, which is probably wise. However, there is no cure for bed-wetting when it is simply the child's will and not a medical condition. Ruling out any medical condition, some children are bed-wetters because of past sexual abuse. It is a tactic to keep themselves dirty and smelly so no one will want to have sex with them. For others it is a way to relieve stress, and for others it is a way to drive their parents crazy (e.g., you can't control what goes in and comes out of their bodies).

Children who are bed-wetters for no apparent medical reason should be responsible for cleaning up their own bedding (including washing and remaking the bed). Parents should enforce this chore with kindness and empathy, but no shaming. We found futons to be good deterrents because they absorb the urine and continue to smell for a while, even after washing. Children who can control their bladders will usually do so if they are going to have to sleep with that consequence. Children who can control their bladders but choose not to are often destructive with their urine. They will urinate on furniture, on the floor, in their clothes. One of my children would urinate out the window. As a result, the urine ate through the paint and the wood of the window sill. Children who purposely urinate and defecate in places other than the toilet (e.g., in the heating vents, in the plants, in the bath tub, etc.) need to clean up the mess. Usually they require additional preventive and interventive measures to curb this undesirable behavior.

Destruction of property: Traumatized children destroy their own, as well as other people's property, in part because they have little respect for people, and even less so for property. However, a less sociopathic reason stems from arrested play development. The child is stuck in the destruction mode of play and has not yet found joy in creating and mastering. These are often the same children who draw a line on a piece of paper and expect rave reviews for their minimal efforts. Limiting their property, as well as access to other's property, is a good preventive measure. These children should not have the bedroom with the designer furniture under the mistaken notion that if nice things surround them they will not be destructive. Better this child's room be kept sparse with things of little value, until the destruction stops. You can reward the child with new things when they have been earned.

Aggression towards self often includes picking at scabs and bug bites until they are bloody and infected, wearing shoes without socks to cause blisters, cutting one's own arms and legs with sharp objects, head-banging, gorging or starving, or setting themselves up to be abused (sexually and physically). The cause of such self-abuse is multifaceted and is almost always a reflection of the unworthiness they perceived from their abusive parents. Self-abuse is highly resistant to intervention. Stopping it may only serve to displace the anger onto others. (e.g., a child stops picking at herself but then becomes physically aggressive towards others).

Annoying Behaviors

Children depend upon their parents for self-definition. In fact, very young children have few means of learning about themselves other than through experiences with their parents. When the early environment is valid and reliable, the self-definition will be positive and will accurately reflect the child's own perceptions of self. The child's internalization of this congruence results in relaxed, contented, and authentic behaviors. Conversely, when the early environment is invalid and unreliable, the self-definition will be negative and will not accurately reflect the child's own perceptions of self. The result is myriad annoying behaviors.

Questioning: Many children whose environments did not accurately reflect who they thought they were are eternally confused and constantly question their own perceptions. These children are often the ones who repeatedly ask questions to which they already know the answers (e.g., "Is it raining out?" while staring at a rain drenched window). They also question almost all parental or authoritative directives (parent: "Put your shoes on now." child: "You want me to put my shoes on now?" or, "Why, do I have to put my shoes on now?"). Some practitioners and parents believe this is a controlling behavior, but it may also be due in part to missing ego capacities in the child.

Other children ask nonsense questions so that if the parent answers the child, the child can confirm that the parent is stupid. Or, if the parent ignores the child, the child can confirm that the parent is unresponsive. Either way, the child has set up the parent to fail (in the child's eyes) so that the child can justify not falling in love with the parent.

Related to asking nonsense questions is the constant requesting of information or the questioning of what the parent is doing. One mother told me "It's like being drilled all day long by my mother-in-law." Another parent referred to it as having a back seat driver: "Where are we going? When are we going to be there? Why are you turning here? Who's going to be there? Why didn't you put gas in the car before? How old is this seat belt?" Notice that the answers to these questions would not give the child information he needs to have. When the parent attempts to answer all of these questions, as if the child deserves to know the answers, the child is reassured that the parent is inadequate and thinks, "I am wise not to trust her." I advise parents to reply to such questions with "I'll let you know," or "Lucky you, you don't have to worry about any of that," or "Won't it be great when you trust me to take care of these things!"

Not following directions or listening to instructions: Traumatized children's victimizers taught them that adults say one thing and do another. Thus, these children assume that all adults are just as confused as their parents were. Therefore, a traumatized child will pay little attention to a parent's overt behaviors, directions and instructions and, instead, try to interpret what they think the adult really means. Or, the child will anticipate what the parent will say or want, often jumping the gun or getting it wrong. For adults who say exactly what they mean and expect children to wait for instructions, this is quite frustrating. These children often appear not to be listening when spoken to (they look away or distract themselves), do the opposite of what you asked, question what you are saying or asking, or come back and ask you to repeat the instruction. One parent told me it's like "being told by your child everyday that you are stupid and you don't know what you really mean to say and, oh, by the way, you are doing a lousy parenting job."

Sneaky: Once again these children learned from the best - their parents. They are like ghosts. You tell them to sit. You turn your back, and they're gone. They are often where they are not supposed to be and are amazingly adept at knowing your whereabouts at all times. They have the biggest ears in the house, except if you are giving them face-to-face instructions (see above). When one of our children was abusing another child in our home late at night, the abusing child knew how to avoid all of the creaky floorboards between the two bedrooms. That's why alarms are important appliances in a house with unknown traumatized children.

A parent once asked me if placing an alarm on her foster child's bedroom door, and not her birth child's door, would make the foster child feel different. I reminded her that the foster child already feels different, and we should not pretend otherwise. The alarm helps to guarantee safety for all members of the family and helps the foster child feel safe. She will know if anyone is coming uninvited into her room. Also, an alarm might prevent her from doing anything she might regret later (e.g., abusing another child).

Attention seeking: It's true that none of us gets enough attention for positive behaviors and only infants receive massive amounts of attention just for existing. However, it appears that many traumatized children are addicted to attention seeking. Many of their attention seeking behaviors are extremely annoying and intrusive (e.g., giggling, noisemaking, asking inane questions, doing the opposite of what everyone else is doing {e.g., wearing winter clothes in summer and summer clothes in winter}, commenting, taking numerous sight seeing tours around the house under the guise of going to the bathroom, getting a drink of water, or looking for something). Interestingly, while their behaviors are intrusive, they fear intrusiveness from others and shun intimacy. They may think they want attention, but as soon as others avail themselves with help and interactions, the children retreat or defend with some insufferable or annoying behavior so they won't be "had."

But fear of aloneness compels them once again to seek attention (aloneness, without distractions like TV or electronic toys, may evoke the child's profound sense of being bad or evil). And because they don't know how to hold attention and feel fulfilled by the parent-child relationship, they will settle for having an audience.

Some people would perceive these attention getting behaviors as misbehavior. But, from an object relations perspective, the child is not misbehaving, but rather is attempting to "check in" or "connect" like a toddler. However, toddlers check-in to reassure themselves that their mothers still love them and that their mothers are still nearby. They are already confident of their own existence. Conversely, traumatized children check-in to reassure themselves of their own existence, not just their mothers. Unfortunately, traumatized children need to check-in and connect quite often because they are so consumed with anxiety in the uncertainty and purity of their own existence. They devise some very creative (usually obnoxious) ways to check-in and connect in hopes of not revealing their fears of non-existence or evilness.

Preying on naïve adults: I was once in an elevator with my then nine year old child, and a fellow grad student when my child went right up to this virtual stranger, wrapped her arms around her neck, and gave her a great big hug with a radiant smile. In response to this bizarre action my fellow grad student did what most well meaning adults would do -- she hugged my child back and said "how sweet" while I stood in the corner giving her the cut-throat hand signal. I have heard many horror stories from parents of how their children buddy up to other adults, schmooze them, snuggle with them, talk eloquently while gazing into their eyes, engage them in fantasy play, and talk them into buying the child anything from a pack of gum to a play station. What's worse, these actions are often done while the child is throwing "glaring daggers" or "I-got-you looks" at the parents.

And why wouldn't these children take advantage of adults? Most adults are well socialized in how to treat children (especially those that are not their own). They are kind and sweet, sympathetic, non-critical, and indulging. They are usually liberal with praise and have low expectations. In other words, they are just the opposite of how we are after living with a traumatized child for an extended period of time. It's a sneaky way to get their needs met, but you can hardly blame the child. Although some adults may think I am a royal B----, I now step right in and tell the adults they are being played. Then I redirect my child away from the situation while saying "Nice try."

Lack of contentment and calmness: Typically, traumatized children were exposed to less than happy and calm environments during their early years of development. As a result, their brains were organized in ways to accommodate chaos, and their bodies responded with hyper-vigilance. That is why traumatized children are often diagnosed with ADHD, not necessarily because they are hyperactive but because they are hyper-vigilant (e.g., looking over their shoulder, watching everyone else like a hawk). These children are restless and often want what everyone else has, but show no honest interest in these things (e.g., a child playing video games is working the controls on his game but his eyes are on the video game next to his). Many of these children use the same word regarding controlled or solitary activities -- "boring." Traumatized children will usually go out of their way to distract themselves and others from activities or interests just for the purpose of creating chaos and avoiding "boredom."

Contrariness comes in direct and indirect forms. An example of direct contrariness is when the parent says, "It's cold out. You must be freezing," and the child replies, "I'm hot." An example of indirect contrariness is when the parent says, "It's really raining hard out there," and the child says, "Not that hard Mom, not as hard as it was the other day." It's as if the child is thinking "I can only define myself by disagreeing with everything you say and do, so I must position myself to be your opposite." Contrariness is one safe way traumatized children can form an identity. Non-traumatized children identify with the parent and often work hard to copy that parent's behavior and words. But traumatized children fear the implications of identifying with a parent or any adult and internalizing their values. So, still needing an identity, they do the next best thing -- the opposite.

Eating: Eating problems range from picky eating to eating inedible things like paper or crayons. But some less subtle eating issues include arranging the food on the plate (e.g., spreading out spaghetti in straight lines, eating foods in order, not allowing different foods to touch each other on the plate), being the last one to finish, expecting parent to cajole them into finishing, and messy eating (all over face and floor). Sometimes traumatized children eat this way because they were never taught otherwise. Some do it because it bothers the parents and controls the situation. Still others may be compulsive. Using "Love and Logic" techniques work very well with eating issues.

Inauthenticity: Traumatized children are often described as chameleon like -- they change with the wind. They say what they think others want to hear; their likes and dislikes alternate between congruence and incongruence with other people's likes or dislikes, depending on what the child believes to be the benefit to her at any given moment. Some believe chameleon behavior is not a choice, but rather that the child really cannot identify her own thoughts and feelings. Some believe that the child doesn't actually have any of her own thoughts and feelings.

From an object-relations perspective, the child is simply presenting a false self to protect the true self from exploitation and annihilation.

Inauthenticity is exhibited by what we call in our home "game playing." The games are performed because the children don't want you to know that they have needs, they fear being turned down, or they don't want to feel beholden to the parent should the parent satisfy their needs. Because they do not interact honestly they are very imaginative in their manipulations, like copying others, hinting and baiting (e.g., "Sure would be a good day to play baseball."), creating elaborate explanations to answer simple "yes" or "no" questions, and giving the deer in the headlights look when asked questions that beg an explanation. The frequency with which traumatized children exhibit inauthentic behaviors ranges from every interaction to only some interactions in specific domains such as care taking needs.

Constant noise making: This comes in the form of humming, chattering, talking to others under one's breath, talking to oneself under one's breath, or providing a running commentary on everything and everyone in the house. Some of the reasons for this odd and annoying behavior include (1) the child is keeping himself company, (2) the child cannot tolerate the parent's attention to be anywhere else but on the child. (3) the child is reminding the parent that she, the child, still exists (every two seconds), (4) the child is controlling the parent and the situation. The traumatized child who makes constant noise usually asks many stupid or obvious questions as well.

Bossy or know-it-all: These children often boss around others (parents) to control and restrict them, but they don't parent themselves very well. They are in essence all id (instinct) and no superego (conscience) regarding their own actions, but they are quick to judge and condemn the actions of others (e.g., tattle-tails on others even though the tattle-taler often partakes in the same behaviors). The goal of these children is not to teach other people right from wrong, but to prevent others from doing or getting something that they don't get to do or have (e.g. if he stands on a chair, then I should get to stand on a chair too, and if I can't do it he shouldn't get to do it either, so I'll tell on him even though I just did it). Know-it-all children operate under the premise that others can't know anything that they don't know, so, therefore, they must know it all.

Exaggeration of abilities and knowledge (e.g., I can climb that mountain, I can drive a car, I know all my times tables) is common in six to ten year olds because they fail so often at new things. If they didn't exaggerate they might just quit altogether and never achieve mastery in anything. But these children demonstrate real abilities and knowledge as well, and don't feel they will die from embarrassment if they get tested on their times tables and mess up a few. For traumatized children being in-the-know is a critical belief to maintain superiority and independence. For them, saying, "I think…." is equal to, "I know." In-the-know children are often disrespectful to adults correcting them, challenging them, or being argumentative.

The Negative vs. Positive Behavior Paradox

After working with hundreds of parents who live with traumatized children I came to the realization that to truly understand the thoughts and actions of these children it is insufficient to only identify their negative sides. However, I found the research in this area of study to be quite lacking.

The way most people think of behavior is to picture positive and negative behaviors on opposite ends of a spectrum. In this conceptualization, the more negative behaviors manifested the fewer positive behaviors manifested, and vice versa, the more positive behaviors manifested the fewer negative behaviors manifested.

Negative ———————————————— Positive

However, this is not an adequate conceptualization because in fact all people manifest a variety of positive and negative behaviors at the same time. Therefore, a better conceptualization is to picture negative and positive behaviors on two separate continuums, each ranging from high to low, as opposed to a single continuum with negative on one end and positive on the other. This means for example, that a child may manifest many negative behaviors and many positive behaviors. It also means that another child may manifest very few negative behaviors and very few positive behaviors.

Positive
Low ———————————————— High

Negative
Low ———————————————— High

This is an important distinction for several reasons. First, almost all behavior assessment tools measure the quantity and frequency of occurrence of negative behaviors, but have no means of accounting for the quantity and frequency of positive behaviors (or lack thereof). They (the tools) are assuming that if there is a plethora of negative behaviors that the positive behaviors do not exist, or are not important. However, positive behaviors reveal healthy family functioning. Without knowledge of what these are and how often they occur how can we truly measure family functioning or relationship satisfaction?

Secondly, because all children manifest some negative behaviors, and parents still love, value, and care for them, perhaps it is the quantity and frequency of positive behaviors that actually predict relationship quality as opposed to the quantity and frequency of negative behaviors. In other words, would a parent-child relationship in which the child is manifesting many negative behaviors plus many positive behaviors be of higher quality than a relationship in which the child was manifesting few negative behaviors but few to no positive behaviors? I predict the answer to this question is "Yes."

Furthermore, I contend that it is actually the lack of positive behaviors (the function of healthy parent-child relationships) that is so very problematic for foster and adoptive parents of traumatized children, as opposed to the plethora of negative behaviors. The negative behaviors that are occurring can be somewhat controlled and perhaps diminished/changed. It's very hard and time consuming, but it can be accomplished. But how do parents control what is not occurring -- with what is not being given? How do parents interact with a child who does not love or care about the parents?

Many children are difficult to parent; it seems almost inherent in the fact of being a child. However, most children give so much back to the relationship (positive behaviors) parents find the job of raising them fairly worthwhile and satisfying. It is a complementarily reciprocal relationship. And, even when some children's negative behaviors are quite pronounced, perhaps they are more bearable because authentic positive behaviors are also present.

But many traumatized children fail to manifest pro-family behaviors, attitudes and beliefs, while manifesting a plethora of negative behaviors, attitudes and beliefs. These manifestations make sense given that traumatized children were not exposed to positive family functioning in their birth homes, and therefore their negative engagement behaviors, although adaptive, became hard wired over time, and their positive social engagement capacities were sorely damaged, or not activated at all. However, while it makes sense, it also makes the job of raising them fairly worthless and unsatisfying. There is nothing reciprocal about these relationships.

A third reason the concept of dual continuums is important is for understanding that reducing negative behaviors does not automatically result in increasing positive behaviors. That is, it appears that helping traumatized children to reduce the quality and quantity of their negative behaviors through appropriate parenting strategies and/or medication does not automatically increase or activate their positive spectrum of behaviors. This further helps to explain the lack of parent satisfaction in these relationships and the high incidence of placement disruptions.

Of course, a dual continuum concept begs the question, "What positive behaviors do parents expect from children that make raising them worth the time, money, and energy?" There are a variety of tools that assess children's negative behaviors (e.g., Child Behavior Check List, RADQ). However, at this time there is no standardized tool (that I am aware of) that lists the positive behaviors or that measures the frequency of positive behaviors (or lack thereof). Without such a tool, there is no valid means of understanding exactly what foster and adoptive parents of traumatized children are not receiving in the relationship (what these children don't bring into the parent-child relationship).

To create such a tool I conducted a study in which I asked seventy parents of non-traumatized children to list five behaviors or traits their children bring into the parent-child relationship that makes them happy, satisfied, or proud to be a parent. After removing many redundant answers and personal attributes/traits (e.g., pretty, intelligent) over 100 "exclusive" behaviors were left and were then sorted into categories. To review the complete survey tool see Appendix A.

The survey tool is still in the preliminary stages. Yet to come is the resorting of content for redundancy to ensure exclusivity of behaviors, and then testing it on different populations. After standardization, the tool will be used for prediction and diagnosis, in addition to description. As it is, the tool can only be used for descriptive purposes, such as (1) a companion to behavior checklists when assessing child functioning and relationship quality of traumatized children and their significant others, (2) a tool to educate and support parents, and (3) a tool to inform therapeutic practice.

For example, when assessing the parent-child relationships of traumatized children the tool can be used to (1) identify both the negative and positive behaviors that are, and are not, being demonstrated by the child as reported by the parents, (2) identify parents' perceptions of relationship satisfaction/quality, and (3) note the correlation between satisfaction and the percentage of positive and negative behaviors. If it is clear that the child is giving very little back to the parents in the form of pro-family behaviors, attitudes, and beliefs then alternative strategies for living and treating these children can be developed with the understanding that they are not engaged in parent-child relationships even though they live in family settings (these alternatives will be discussed in the next section on parenting; using the tool to inform therapeutic practice will be discussed in a later section).

PARENTING

Most foster/adoptive parents of traumatized children have three burning questions: "Is my child behaving badly/oddly deliberately or can he just not help it?" "Why is he behaving so badly/oddly?" and "How do I parent a child who is acting badly/oddly?" In the previous sections the first two questions were explored. The simple answer to the first question is "Both." The simple answer to the second question is "Because his birth parent-child relationship was faulty." Now we'll explore the answer to the third question, whose simple answer is "Differently than you would expect."

Parenting Typologies

Over the past fifty years, the research on parenting behaviors and attitudes has culminated in conceptualizations of specific parenting typologies (Amato, 1990; Darling & Steinberg, 1993, Maccoby & Martin, 1983). This research determined that most parenting behaviors and attitudes could be captured under a two-dimensional scheme of support (responsiveness) and control (demandingness) that are separated into high and low levels. The result is four specific parenting styles into which parental behaviors can be categorized.

A parent using parenting behaviors that are very controlling and very supportive is said to have an "authoritative" parenting style; high control and low support = an "authoritarian" parenting style; low control and high support = a "permissive-indulgent" parenting style; low control and low support = a "permissive-neglectful" parenting style.

CONTROL

	Low	High
Low	Permissive Neglectful	Authoritarian
High	Authoritative	Permissive Indulgent

S
U
P
P
O
R
T

Research has demonstrated that each of these categories is correlated with a variety of child outcomes (e.g., academic performance, social skills, moral development), with the authoritative parenting style correlating with the most positive results (see Maccoby & Martin, 1983, for a complete review). Authoritative parents tend to have clear requirements of their children for prosocial, responsible behavior and expect their children to demonstrate self-discipline, quality performance, and a good work ethic, and to help with household duties. They usually have realistic expectations, and teach, guide and assist their children in fulfilling their requirements. And, they do not usually rescue children from consequences of their own choices (natural or logical), or complete tasks for children that they can clearly do themselves.

Authoritative parents typically use reasoning and problem-solving techniques that enlist the thinking of the child in order to achieve compliance. Authoritative parents' expect that: (1) they will have to compromise (but believe they should have the final say), (2) children can and will participate in decision making, and (3) children's thinking abilities and contributions, at whatever level, should be recognized and valued.

Authoritative parents engage in a system of complementary reciprocity in which they respond to their children's needs and expect their children to respond to parental demands. And, in fact, children raised in authoritative home environments are more likely and willing to respond positively to the demands of their parents compared to children raised in other home environments. Authoritative home environments also employ a mechanism for systematic change over time to accommodate children's increasing cognitive abilities. The parents are not necessarily relinquishing control, but, instead, provide a continuous pattern of democracy in which changes in the level of choices made available to the child, and the construction of the learning environment, expand as the child's cognitive abilities expand. Such patterns include co-regulation, reciprocity of control, joint problem solving, and cooperation (Youniss, 1980).

Authoritarian parents, on the other hand, believe in controlling the child's thoughts and behaviors, and forcing/coercing the child into compliance. They typically expect (1) not to compromise with their children, (2) children not to participate in decision-making, and (3) children's thoughts and feelings to be irrelevant. Authoritarian parenting behaviors and attitudes correlate with children's lower academic performance, poorer peer relationships, and greater dependency needs than children raised in authoritative home environments (Brody & Shaffer, 1982;

Maccoby & Martin, 1983).

Permissive-indulgent parents are as the typology title implies. They: (1) almost always give in to the demands of the child, (2) over estimate and over value children's thinking abilities and contributions, (3) reward too lavishly and rescue children from responsibilities because they are over invested in making their children happy or impressing their neighbors, and (4) sometimes are resented by their children who perceive their parents' love as not genuine.

Outcomes of children raised in permissive-indulgent home environments are often less positive than those of children raised in authoritative home environments. They tend to be more like those raised in authoritarian home environments. Some resemble those raised in permissive-neglectful home environments, which can be quite poor (permissive-neglectful parents are the ones we typically associate with being involved with social services for abusing or neglecting their children; their parenting attitudes and behaviors are discussed later). One difference between those children raised in permissive-indulgent home environments and those raised in permissive-neglectful home environments appears to be levels of aggression; children raised in permissive-indulgent homes show less aggressive tendencies than children raised in permissive-neglectful homes, presumably because the latter are much more likely to be exposed to violence and abuse in the home.

Sadly, over the past 20 years in the United States, the number of parents using a permissive-indulgent parenting style has increased greatly, most probably due to greater affluence, a hedonistic cultural norm, and a societal merging of adulthood and childhood (see Neil Postman

"The Disappearance of Childhood, 1994). Permissive-indulgent parents are often invested in being their child's friend, and in so doing deprive the child of an adult image to juxtapose his own personality formation. By being childish themselves, the parents convince the child he cannot rely on them for control or protection (Bettelheim, 1950). This may explain, at least in part, why relationship problems amongst children and adolescents in general are on the rise.

It's logical to assume that because an authoritative parenting style is so successful with non-traumatized children, it will be equally effective with traumatized children. However, this parenting style is successful because the children are securely attached. They "buy-in" to the relationship hierarchy, and they feel a sense obligation to the relationship. Authoritative parents will soon become frustrated with their children's lack of reciprocity, myriad annoying and distancing behaviors, and inability to learn from consequences.

All parents of traumatized children must incorporate information, adjust beliefs, and gain skills to be successful. There are many excellent books available that teach effective parenting of traumatized children (some are provided at the end of this chapter). Much of the parenting information and ideas I provide will supplant these books and reinforce many of their ideas. However, I will also present a model for working and living with traumatized children that is quite unique, based on the structure and function of parent-child relationships as well as the dual continuums of positive and negative behavior I presented in the previous sections of the book. But first, the basics.

FYI

Discipline vs. Punishment

Discipline is a direct training or learning experience that, when done correctly, develops self-control, self-esteem, moral character, responsible behavior, emotional IQ, and orderly conduct in an individual or a society. Discipline can be experienced as positive or negative, but almost always entails acceptance or submission to authority or control. Punishment is interceptive, which means it happens after the misbehavior. It can range from mild (induce discomfort, shame, guilt) to severe (physical or emotional pain and suffering). Most parents use removal of privileges or objects, time out, or spanking as forms of punishment.

Discipline Problems vs. Behavior Problems

Discipline problems lie within the adult's responsibility and control. Discipline problems (non-compliance, misbehavior) occur when the parents (or other supervising adults) have not structured the child's environment for success, or when the parents are inconsistent (in their expectations and/or consequences), non-responsive, or inaccessible. When adults adjust their behaviors and attitudes, often children with discipline problems can be brought under control in as few as three to seven days. Conversely, behavior problems lie within the child. These are persistent behaviors that do not disappear, even with the best parenting, although good parenting can help to control the behaviors. Typical behavior problems include impulsivity, inattentiveness, and other behaviors associated with organic or physiological brain dysfunctions (e.g., ADHD, Fetal Alcohol Syndrome/Effect), and/or immature behaviors associated with missing capacities in object relations.

It does not behoove a parent or teacher to expect a child with a behavior problem to control himself; they will only feel relentless frustration and will probably take it out on the child. Instead, expect that this is a behavior the adult will have to control (I'll explain how, momentarily), and that it may take a very long time (years) to transfer these control skills to the child. For example, think of a behavior problem as something the child was born with, like poor eyesight. No amount of punishing or controlling is going to fix this problem. Glasses will help. However, the parent will be responsible for taking the child for regular eye check-ups, teaching him how to care for his glasses, and restricting him from activities where his glasses might break. The goal, of course, is that by the time he is eighteen, and walking out the door into adulthood, he will be ready and able to take full responsibility for the care of his own eyes and glasses.

Many parents of traumatized children struggle with whether to classify a child's misbehavior as a discipline problem or a behavior problem. The best way to know for sure is to change the home environment. If the child's behavior stops or improves, it is likely a discipline problem. If the child's behavior remains unchanged, but more in control (by the parent), and the parent is acting consistently, it is likely a behavior problem.

Punishment vs. Consequences

Just as people confuse punishment with discipline, so, too, do they confuse punishment with consequences (although these are more similar as they most often take place after the misbehavior). However, while punishment usually inflicts pain and suffering in hopes of stemming a bad behavior, consequences do not have to hurt to teach. For example, spanking a child or removing his bicycle for a week is a punishment for sassing his mom. Consequences for sassing his mom might be brushing mom's hair, drawing her a picture, or doing one of her chores (i.e., pay back meanness with niceness). Typical differences between punishment and consequences are:

Punishment	Consequence
emotional	non emotional / matter of fact
physically painful	not physically painful
humiliating	not humiliating
arbitrary	planned
sometimes illogical	logical / natural
removal of object/ privilege	adding of task/responsibility

One way punishment and consequences are similar is that they both can restrict the child, but the logic is different. For example, after exhibiting poor behavior in the supermarket, a parent may restrict a child by sending him to his room. This would be considered a punishment. But if a child is unmanageable in public places a parent may choose not to take the child to these places until he can demonstrate some restraint. This is restrictive as well -- a consequence of the child's lack of maturity, not a punishment for being bad. Furthermore, the consequence is being used as a preventive measure (as in discipline). Parents and children benefit when parents "listen" to what children's behavior is telling them (usually and underlying unmet need) rather than expecting children to perform at things they may not be ready for and then punishing them for bad behavior.

Parental Expectations

When parenting traumatized children it is helpful to remember: Trust is the first psychosocial skill we learn as infants. When infants and young children are not fed and changed on a regular basis, when they are abused, neglected, or abandoned by their parents they learn to mistrust them, and, therefore, the world. Their brains don't set up in sensible, organized patterns equipped for learning. They don't experience myriad positive interactions nor do they have a sense of belonging to something greater than themselves. As a result, they can develop attachment / relationship problems that affect every aspect of their development. Almost all foster/older-adopted children manifest one-to-many attachment / relationship problems because they experienced inefficient or improper parental responsiveness in their early years of life. Without this constant reminder, you will burn out fast. Here are a few expectations to keep in mind:

1) Expect to feel disillusioned. Power & Krause (1995) refer to the process of parenting older adopted children as "shrouded by myth and dominated by emotion." Their interviews with adoptive parents revealed that most adoptive parents believed that adopting a child would be a rewarding experience, and were therefore not prepared for the actual day-to-day problems, and immense emotional toll it takes to raise a traumatized child. Many parents have difficulty reconciling their fantasies about adoptive family life with the realities. They often blame themselves for the child's failure to respond, and feel terrible that they do not love the child, or that they feel so angry towards the child all of the time. Many parents,

however, find relief and solutions from information and support from other adoptive parents.

2) Expect punishment to be fairly ineffective in making permanent changes in behavior. Punishment (removal of an object or privilege, time out, spanking) is an unsuccessful tool for four reasons. First, if the child has access to many material distractions, removing one item or grounding the child will do little good. You take her bike, but she has a dozen other things she can play with. You send him to his room, but he's got a TV and VCR in his room. Second, unless you plan on abusing this child more than he has already been abused (which no one would condone) you can't hurt him with a spanking. The only thing you will teach him is that all adults who say they love him will hurt him. Third, the goal of many traumatized children is to thwart your efforts so they can justify not trusting you or falling in love with you. Punishment to them is an acceptable by-product to this end. Finally, what good is punishing children who are already doing such a spectacular job of punishing themselves?

3) Expect to control the child's behaviors, but not necessarily to change them. Most traumatized children have few to many behavior problems. Focusing on these behaviors in hopes of having them change will be harmful to you and to the child. One of my children had been told by many previous foster parents that his bad behaviors were preventing him from being adopted and that he must behave or else. I told him that his behaviors were not bad they were immature and no different than any three year old child (he was eleven). I also told him to stop worrying about his behaviors because it was my job to help him control himself just as it would be if he were actually three years old, and, if he messed up it was probably my fault for

not controlling him well enough.

This relieved him from the pressure of having to change those "bad" behaviors and gave me all the power. For example, when taking him out to dinner for the first time I prepared him by saying, "Don't worry if you can not control yourself in the restaurant. That just means it was too soon for you to be out and it will be Daddy's and my fault for taking you out before you were ready. If you do get too loud or restless, you can always sit out in the car and wait for us and we can bring you some food to go." He actually behaved appropriately that night, but we did not expect him to act consistently appropriate from then on, which, of course, he did not. Parents who expect their child to change behavior problems will be very disappointed. And parents who do not take responsibility for controlling these behaviors will set their child up for failure time and time again.

4) Along those same lines: Do not expect your values and morals to be internalized by the child or generalized to other situations for years to come. Your child's behavior problems are always present. When he is relaxed and when he is stressed these are the ones he will use spontaneously and automatically because those brain connections have long been established and will only be superseded by different ones after years of training. Only with outside influences (supervision, reminders, consequences reinforcement) will a child make the effort to choose alternative behaviors (remember the sledgehammer and chisel?). For example, I was observing a child one afternoon in his school. He new me and knew my expectations of him and what the consequences would be if he misbehaved. He proceeded to act exactly as he should, surprising his teacher who just that morning had confronted him on a variety of

behavior problems. I asked him later why he only behaved when I was watching him and he said, "Because you were watching me."

5) Do not expect your child to act responsibly or to take responsibility for wrongdoing. Being responsible means doing things right the first time, taking responsibility means once you have messed up you accept the consequences. Even when you have done a good job of helping children control their behaviors, there will still be many times when they will act irresponsibly. They must be held responsible for how they do act if they are ever to learn cause and effect thinking. Even if the lesson never results in changes in behavior, they will know that negative things (unpleasant or inconvenient) happen to them as a result of their own poor choices.

6) Expect to feel conflicted about what you think is good parenting and what is good parenting for traumatized children. For example, parents often tell me that they try to treat their adopted children the same as their birth children, but it doesn't always seem fair. That is, they bestow on their adopted children the same privileges given to their birth children even though their adopted children's behaviors are so much worse. Although treating birth and adoptive children the same makes intuitive sense, it actually teaches a traumatizing child that he has earned what more giving, socially responsible children receive. That is what is not fair or logical. Each child needs to be treated according to what his behavior suggests he has earned, needs, and can handle. Equality of resources and even outcomes is not the goal.

7) Do not expect to make your child's life easier, if he doesn't want it to be easier. If your traumatized child decides to bend over and purposely run headlong into a brick wall (figuratively speaking) every day, there is

nothing you should do about it. You could pad all of the walls, remind him how painful it is, and how sad it makes you feel when he does these things. However, he will simply find the one spot you forgot to pad, work harder at proving to you it's not painful, and be angry with you for feeling bad for him. You will not accomplish your goal because he is bound and determined to do things his way, even if it makes his life more difficult.

8) Expect to mess up. We all do. None of us is consistently on target, well rested, patient, or in the mood 100% of the time. Seventy-five percent of the time is a good goal. Always remember that parenting behaviors such as screaming, yelling, scolding, correcting, answering dumb questions, and intimidation make you feel bad and are mostly a waste of your time. Ask yourself if your behavior is good for you? Stop talking and take action. Make the child's behavior a problem for her not for you.

Parenting Skills

The pop literature on parenting (non-traumatized children) is surprisingly interconnected and unified as to which parenting skills are important in raising children. Four strategies recur in one form or another in most of this literature: Prevention, Teaching Responsibility, Behavior Modification, and Emotion Coaching.

Prevention: Essentially, prevention means removing obstacles to success prior to failure. This principle is particularly useful in parenting children with behavior problems.

a. remove temptations - this may mean locking up food, TV's, remote controls, toys and other items you do not wish the child to gain access to.

b. set clear, concise limits and boundaries - e.g., no noise making in the car, no eating in the living room, no going into anyone else's room.

c. establish family rules (for whole family, including parents) - e.g., no hitting, no lying, and no stealing.

d. create a quiet, safe, organized environment - watch TV sparingly, keep bedrooms austere (minimal toys & clothes until children prove responsible with them), have a place for everything & everything in its place.

e. create routines - bedtime & mealtime rituals, cleaning schedules.

Many traumatized children, however, will work hard to create chaos where you have created order. This does not mean you should give in and let go of your principles. Rather, you will use the next three principles to reinforce the order.

Teach Responsibility: Preventive techniques will only go so far. Your children will mess up. Therefore, consequences are essential; rules are only as good as the consequences you use to back them up. Because punishment does not typically work, consequences should be in the form of added responsibilities - also called restitution (paying back for damage done) - as opposed to loss of privilege or object, time out, or spanking. Of course, while children are performing these added chores they may miss out on other activities, particularly if they don't perform the chore right away or right the first time. But that should be of no consequence to the parent.

a. Natural consequences (brought about by the situation): if the child acts mean no one will play with her; if the child doesn't wear his coat, he will be cold.

b. Logical consequences (ordered by the adult):

restitution = admit, apologize, make amends (with $, or chores, or doing something nice for the offended person).

c. Share control: all children want control but given too much they control you, given too little they feel incompetent and frustrated. Giving appropriate choices allows children control over things they should have control over, and instills a sense of responsibility and self-efficacy.

d. Do not argue with an illogical child, you will only look foolish and draw attention to your behavior and away from the child's behavior.

Behavior Modification: Behavior modification techniques like charts and stickers are often ineffective with traumatized children because they enjoy sabotaging your efforts at getting them to behave, or are purposely inconsistent so as to prove from one day to the next that they really are bad terrible children and don't deserve rewards. However, the following behavior modification ideas are a must for any parenting plan.

a. Ignore negative attention-seeking behaviors, but truly ignore them. Don't say, "I'm ignoring you." Don't roll your eyes or huff and puff.

b. Acknowledge negative attention seeking behaviors, but do not nag the child about them -

praise: "You do that well."
clap: "That's the best fit you've thrown all day."
video tape: "Wait, let me put this on tape so I can
              always remember it."

c. give positive attention for acceptable or prosocial behaviors and on progress, but expect a relapse when you do. Also don't overdo praise when a child does what is expected.

Emotion-Coaching: One aspect of parenting behavior that is not subsumed under the two-dimensional scheme of support and control is referred to as "emotion-coaching" (Gottman, Katz, & Hooven, 1996). Emotion coaching entails parents' awareness of their emotions, their child's emotions, and their interpretations and interventions regarding these emotions during parent-child interactions. Emotion-coaching parents use "scaffolding-praising," a skill that goes beyond the warm and structured authoritative typology and fosters emotional connectedness with children. Furthermore, they use little derogation, a behavior that increases emotional distance.

Emotion coaching is a skill that all foster/adoptive parents must acquire for several reasons. First, traumatized children are masters at pushing parental buttons. Without self-emotional awareness and control, attention will be drawn away from the child's behavior and towards the parent's behaviors. The child will use this as a diversion from focusing on his own emotions. Also, repeated exposure to conflict and drama in which your emotions are triggered and not controlled can leave you feeling traumatized by the child. Second, if traumatized children are to gain self-control and social competence, it will be up to you to acknowledge, label, and accept their emotions. Third, emotion coaching can help to create a more attachment-friendly environment. When your emotions are out of control the child may perceive you as weak and therefore refuse to trust or connect with you. Conversely, when the child knows you can control your own emotions, and that he is safe when expressing strong emotions, the environment is optimal for a healthy relationship to form.

a. Identify and acknowledge feelings, needs and wants; name the emotion:

"You must be feeling so frustrated right now."

"What do you want?"

"How can you get it?"

b. Guide the processing of feelings but do not solve the problem. Mirror feelings, ask questions to clarify, give advice cautiously. Ask the child what she thinks.

c. Draw attention to the four main emotions that help build a conscience:

Pride:	let him know what makes you proud
Empathy:	explain how his behavior affects others
Guilt:	encourage feeling bad for acting badly
Embarrassment:	normalize- Anyone would feel that way

d. Acknowledge excessive shame that prevents conscience building. Separate "bad" behavior from the "good self"

e. Prompt the child by saying what you think he feels and then check it out with him: "You look sad, are you feeling sad?"

f. Role-play or act out conflictual situations both before and after the fact. Include how the child felt or might feel, and what the child did or should do about it.

g. Use humor to lighten the moment but not to ridicule the child.

h. Use and teach "I" statements

I feel	(emotion)
When you	(behavior)
Because	(reason)
What I want is	(need/want)

Developmental Reparenting

A fifth strategy specifically aimed at parenting the traumatized child is called "developmental reparenting" Because traumatized children's developmental domains (physical, cognitive, social/emotional) are far less in sync than are those of non-traumatized children, the pattern of democracy parents create and the mechanism for systematic change they adopt must accommodate traumatized children's lowest functioning domain. In almost all cases, their lowest functioning domain is emotional development. Therefore, a parent who institutes this strategy changes the level of choices made available to the child and the construction of the learning environment, in accordance with the child's emotional abilities, as opposed to her cognitive or physical ability.

The goal of developmental reparenting is to encourage a stronger attachment between parent and child. Therefore, developmental reparenting requires parenting behaviors typically reserved for infants and toddlers such as contingent responsiveness, accessibility and availability, complete acceptance, care giving. The parent engages in many activities that respect the child's emotional age such as rocking the child like an infant while using eye contact, touch (skin-to-skin contact), smiling and laughter, and sometimes sugar (fed to the child by the parent). Nancy Thomas (1997) refers to this activity as "snuggle time."

In addition, parents sing, recite nursery rhymes, and play hide and seek with the child. Parents and children work together, cooking, putting groceries away, and cleaning the house (once in awhile the parent will ask the child to complete these small activities on her own because it helps the child feel she is giving back to the parent). Finally, the parent does many nurturing and caring tasks for the child, such as brushing her hair and teeth, feeding her, bathing her (or, if the child is older, just washing her hair), and even using baby massage techniques. And, of course, there is lots of hugging and kissing going on.

Relationship Coaching

I am currently experimenting with a new approach for working and living with traumatized children (the unique model I alluded to in the previous sections). As suggested earlier, many traumatized children fail to manifest pro-family behaviors, attitudes and beliefs, while manifesting a plethora of negative behaviors, attitudes and beliefs. In addition, decreasing their negative behaviors does not always result in an increase in these positive behaviors. Again this is due to the fact that negative and positive behaviors may be quite independent from one another.

The negative behaviors tend to be the child's natural response system because they were developed in early childhood to defend against trauma and were then generalized to fit most, if not all, situations with adults; many traumatized children have practiced these negative behaviors for years. Conversely, they have had little experience and practice with positive behaviors, which therefore do not come naturally even when they see these behaviors modeled by others every day. They have no reason to model these behaviors because for the most part their basic needs are being met as well as many of their wants; reciprocating is an unnecessary practice for the relationships they are engaged in. Therefore, there is no impetus for change and no skills for making those changes occur.

Using the survey tool I developed parents and

practitioners can identify the positive behaviors (if any) children do give to the parent-child relationship. A low number of positive behaviors suggests that these children are not actually in parent-child relationships even though they live in family environments, and the surrogate parents are expecting a parent-child relationship. Instead of forcing a family on these children, I suggest providing a living environment model in which they are not assimilated into a family unit until they are ready.

Unfortunately, the belief put forth in most foster/ adoptive parent training programs is: Provide child with caring surrogate parents (foster parents) and a normal family environment and the child will learn appropriate social skills and her passed wounds will heal. In many ways, however, this belief places the cart before the horse, and it will not work for many traumatized children, as I previously explained. The belief I propose is: Provide a restrictive, predictable (needs are met), friendly environment with authoritative coaches trained in social engagement skills and the child may learn to accept them as his/her parents and gain the capacity to live in a normal family environment. The following is an outline comparing the practices used based on these beliefs.

The Traditional Practice
- Include child as if a family member
- Provide love and nurturing
- Protect and serve
- Teach right from wrong (punishment)
- Give minimal assistance with treatment plan
- Give minimal assistance with reunification plan

The Alternative Practice
- Meet child's basic needs, nothing more (food, shelter, clothes, medical care, hygiene products, educational opportunities).
  - Affection is given only in response to the child's demonstration of affection and only in small doses.
- Provide a safe, predictable environment
- Give and allow consequences
  - limit possibilities for negative behaviors (prevention)
  - contain and control child's negative behaviors
  - do not punish wrong or negative behaviors; use consequences instead
- Coach prosocial interactions
- Give maximum assistance with treatment plan
- Give maximum assistance with reunification plan (where applicable)

The alternative belief supports the practice of providing traumatized children who enter a new home an institutional-like environment, referred to by Federici as "structure and rehabilitation" (e.g., adult supervision, law and order, minimal stimulation, no emotional investment {love} or frills), as opposed to a family-like environment (welcoming, accepting, loving, stimulating, indulgent) until the children have demonstrated reciprocation.

The reasons for providing the "structure and rehabilitation" environment are twofold. This environment prevents traumatized children from feeling the immense stress often experienced when having to "pretend" a parent-child relationship and having to fit in to a family-life that is completely foreign to them. Second, this approach prevents traumatized children from their tendency to take from those who so freely give, hence decreasing their opportunities to practice narcissistic behaviors and increasing their opportunities to practice attachment behaviors. To better understand the underpinnings of the "structure and rehabilitation" approach vs. the "love and affection" approach, I strongly recommend that parents and practitioners read *Help for the Hopeless Child* by Ronald Federici (1998).

Included in this practice, however, is what I have come to call "Relationship Coaching." Relationship coaching was developed to answer two problems: (1) child is not reciprocating with the care giver, (2) the negative vs. positive behavior paradox.

Many foster and adoptive parents become utterly exhausted from parenting traumatized children. Many of their efforts are met with opposition and sometimes abuse. But these children can be encouraged towards a parent-child relationship without the emotional and often physical toll, if parents will act as their relationship coach, rather than their parents. Parents are often caught off guard by the traumatized child's emotions and behaviors because the parents are expecting a certain functionality that the child can not perform.

A coach, on the other hand does not have the same level of emotional investment as a parent and teaches as if the player knows nothing about the game. The coach tells the player what to do and how to do it and evaluates how the game went. A coach is a loyal advisor who provides support, reinforcement, and constructive examples. And a coach wants to bring out the best in others, sees solutions and opportunities, and is a good strategizer. But if the player doesn't follow the rules he is benched. And the coach does not expect to be loved and does not attempt to get his emotional needs met from his players.

This shift in approach lowers the parent's expectation of reciprocity and prevents the child from pretending a parent-child relationship he knows nothing of (Bettelheim,1950). Instead, the relationship coach, contains and controls the child's negative behaviors (through the use of natural and logical consequences) and activates the traumatized child's social engagement circuitry through direct teaching of prosocial engagement, as opposed to passive teaching such as modeling or vicarious learning, or reactive teaching such as punishment and disappointment.

The rationale behind this model is that these children mainly function from their midbrain regions, which means they are almost always living in their trauma and responding to life with defense mechanisms. When we scold them, question them, punish them, or even expect them to interact in a positive way they will retreat to the midbrain and come out fighting.

When we stop scolding, questioning, punishing, and expecting, and instead point out the relationship between what they do and how they feel, and coach positive interactions we are helping them to connect the missing dots (neural pathways) between their midbrains and their frontal lobes (frontal lobe is responsible for reasoning and logic and mediates the emotion center of the midbrain). In essence, the coach becomes the child's frontal lobe, and coaching may help the child shift out of fight or flight mode by activating a higher level response system - the social engagement circuitry (for more information on the social engagement circuitry see Porges, 2003).

In addition, by focusing less on diminishing or changing highly resistant negative "stop" behaviors and focusing more on teaching positive "start" behaviors (pro parent-child relationship and much more pleasant interactions), positive and loving feelings towards the Coaches (parents) may follow.

The following are some examples of how the relationship coach activates the traumatized child's social engagement circuitry by cueing the child's prosocial interactions.

- Apply good cognition to wrong or negative behaviors
  - "You hugged that stranger. You must love her very much."
  - "You are chattering again, you are worried that you don't exist."
  - "You are bossing me around again. You want to control me."
- Coach or cue positive actions that non traumatized children would typically do given a certain situation. The coach says the following to the child:
  - "You hide behind me because a stranger has just come in the room and you are a little scared."
  - "You climb in my lap because you want me to read you a story and you feel all warm inside."
  - "You look me in the eye (or down to the floor) and tell me the truth because you feel bad about what you did."
  - "You come get a hug because you are hurt and need me to help you feel better."

• Coach or cue positive verbal interactions. The coach says to the child: "This is when (or where) you say to me…
  • Coach I feel embarrassed when I do something wrong." "Go"
  • Coach I feel really angry when you tell me what to do." "Go"
  • Coach I don't want to do my chores. I want to make you angry." "Go"
  • Coach It's really hard and scary to be me." "Go"
• Every coaching phrase contains an action and/or a feeling, and many can be based on the positive behaviors found in the survey tool.
• Respond with reciprocal action and/or exaggerated affect
  • positive three-part interactions naturally occur in healthy parent-infant relationships and evoke feelings of love, joy, and comfort.
• If the child does not respond to the cue the…
  • parent does not respond, or
  • parent says to the child, "You can try again later," or
  • parent is unresponsive to the child until the child takes action.

Initially, using this technique will feel very strange to some parents. Parents/coaches sometimes resist coaching because:

a. they insist on being the parents (forcing a parent-child relationship on the child)

b. they believe the child must be punished or else the child is getting away with something.

c. they feel stupid or can't always think of what to say or are afraid they will get it wrong.

However, parents (coaches) who are already using it report...

    a. less conflict and more laughter in the home.
    b. it's the only time positive interactions occur.
    c. a reduction in the child's negative interactions and negative behaviors.
    d. feeling more in control of themselves and their children.
    e.. more spontaneous positive interactions.

When teaching this model, I remind parents that they do not have to be right all the time about the child's emotional state of mind or even the reasons for the child's negative behavior. They just have to be close. The parent/coach is usually a heck of a lot closer to the truth of the child's emotional state and reasons for negative behavior than is the child.

It is important that you, the relationship coach not ask the child any questions, especially those you already know the answer to (which is most of them). Questioning is likely to be perceived by the child as accusatory and will push the child into defense mode. Anytime you are tempted to ask a question, reframe it into a coaching statement. For example:

"Why did you break that toy?" becomes…

This is where you say to me, "Coach, I broke my toy because I was mad." "Go."

"Where were you?" becomes…

This is where you say to me, "Coach, I was hanging out in the bathroom because I didn't want to do my school work." "Go."

"Didn't I tell you to do your chores?" becomes...
This is where you say to me "Coach, I heard you tell me to do my chores but I chose not to do them." "Go."

The relationship coach model gives permission to parents to be parents or to be coaches. In other words, some parents who are highly resistant to being only a "coach" can use the model as a parenting skill they can shift into when being the "parent" is not working (for either them or the child). And, because children will not always comply with what the coach is asking them to do or say, the model recognizes that children need practice and time. There are four basic phases to the relationship coach model:

Phase 1 – Modeling/Opposing: During phase one parents/coaches are likely to receive the most opposition from children to being coached. In this phase children should not be expected to comply. Instead, this is a time of introduction for the child. The coach will model coaching behavior and is simply planting the seed for what is to come. Failure to comply with the coach may be a sign of poor attachment and/or a sign that the child is arrested/ frozen in shame, which is to be expected. As a result, when coached the child's behaviors may escalate as she fends off overwhelming feelings of failure and unworthiness. This can be a topic for coaching at some future point, but not while the child is having a tantrum.

Phase 2 - Shaping/Reluctance: During phase two coaches can expect some compliance from the child but it will probably be with attitude or with a time lapse. For example, the child may repeat after the coach but will do so in a smart alecky way. The coach is to ignore the attitude and provide a positive response as if the child was sincere.

Sometimes the child will not or can not be responsive in the moment, but the coach can check back several minutes or even an hour later and repeat the request. The child may be more compliant at this time. For example, the child fails to thank you for help and when coached refuses to comply. A few minutes later the coach can say to the child, "You look like your ready now. This is where you say to me, Thank you for helping me with that." "Go." Phase two is about practice. The child is usually reluctant but will not typically escalate in emotion or behavior.

Phase 3 – Reinforcing/Internalization: During phase three the child is receptive to coaching and can do so in the moment. The child is now able to demonstrate sincere compliance and willingness to be coached, although he still may not be able to engage on his own. Once the child demonstrates sincere compliance the door will be open for further "cognitive" (reasonable) discussion. This is a good opportunity for the coach to reinforce prosocial interactions.

Phase 4 – Reciprocity/Spontaneity: During this stage the child is able to respond in prosocial ways with little to no encouragement from the coach. The child is engaged with the care giver and can now fully function in a parent-child relationship. Coaching may still be used when necessary, but is used mainly as an adjunct parenting skill.

There is no time schedule to the phases. Coaches will know they are in a different phase by the child's behaviors and reactions to being coached. At no time should children be punished for failure to comply with coaching. The coach simply says "We'll try again later." Also, don't attempt to coach a child who is out of control. The anger curve for many of these children is quick to peak, so it is imperative that all contact in which confrontation is a possibility is approached with coaching as opposed to questioning.

I have had many personal experiences with this model that demonstrate this shift. For example, after repeatedly asking my son to stop chattering I called him into the room and said to him, "Son this is where you say to me, Mom, I am really worried about something." My son's first response was "No I'm not." I did not argue with him, I simply requested that he repeat after me and cued him on the sentence I wanted him to say. He finally said it, well at least partially. Midway through saying "I'm worried about something" he began to cry – much to his surprise. He didn't know he was worried about something and it only dawned on him when he said the words. I then cued him to say "I don't know what to do, can you help me? He repeated this question and then sincerely asked me, "Can you help me?" I had been helping this child for seven years but to him my being able to help was a complete surprise. This was the first time he actually ever asked me for help and we went on to have quite a lovely conversation.

Here's another example. After one of my children said, "Here" and shoved some information about picture taking he received from school under my nose, I coached him in the following way.

"Son, this is where you say to me Mom, I don't know anything about picture taking." "Go."

"Now you say," "Mom, can you help me?" "Go."

After he repeated these two sentences I replied in my best exaggerated Mommy voice, "Yes, I can. I am so happy you asked me. I know a lot about picture taking." This child smiled so broadly at me I had to laugh out loud. He was truly thrilled in the accomplishment of having communicated well with me and having elicited a positive response from me. We then went on to discuss what picture taking at school was all about and had a mutually satisfying interaction – an event that was and is rare without coaching.

If I had been in parent mode I would have said to this child, "Why are you shoving this stuff at me? You need to use better manners if you expect me to buy you pictures." To which he would have denied doing anything wrong and gone off in a huff. We both would have been quite dissatisfied with that interaction.

It would never have dawned on either of these children to engage in these seemingly obvious interactions with a parent. Not because they did not want to, but because they did not know how. Coaching introduces traumatized children to an entirely new way of learning that is non-evasive, non-threatening, and has immediate positive results. Of course, I have introduced this model to parents whose children were quite resistant to being coached. They say things like, "You can't put words in my head." Or, "You can't make me say what I don't want to say." This is true, and I advise parents to validate the child's beliefs while still encouraging them to repeat after the parent/coach. These parents can say, "You are absolutely right, but say it anyway." Or, "This is true, let me know when you are ready."

I believe that the child repeating the parent/coach's words is the most valuable aspect of the coaching model, although I have no data yet to prove why this is so. I theorize that saying the words activates a different part of the brain, the part that allows for constructive evaluation, realization, and reflection. The words in essence are "I statements," fed to the child by the wiser coach because the child can not find the words herself. Once said, the words, and all the feelings and logic they convey, can be discovered

and analyzed, perhaps for the first time, by the child. Saying these specific statements and questions may have a similar therapeutic effect as that found by some clinicians and researchers with client story telling or
writing.

Anyone using this model should remember two things at all times. First, the role and expectations of the coach are different from the role and expectations of the parent. Second, never take for granted that a traumatized child would know how to engage in even the most simple of positive interactions. (And by the way, the relationship coach model can work well with any child).

Parenting from the Trenches

As foster and adoptive parents my husband and I have felt and learned much through the years: some of it was/is bad and some of it was/is good. There are times when we can't stand our children, times when we lose all hope for them, and times when we lose all hope for ourselves. Then, there are the fun times with our children, the times we laugh hysterically at their bizarre ways of being in the world, the times we teach them something new or share new adventures, or the times we actually see progress. Here's what we do and think:

1) It's okay to strongly dislike your children once in a while -- birth parents do. The key is to act lovingly, even when you feel otherwise. If you cannot do what is in the child's best interest because of strong negative emotions, it's time for respite.

2) Be kind: Many traumatized children respond to kindness and punishment in the same way -- with hatred, contempt or distrust. However, being kind (behaviors and tone of voice) makes it more difficult for the child to blame

the parent and forces the child to shoulder alone the responsibility of the problem, or at the very least the negative emotions he alone is feeling. Kindness also makes you feel better about yourself (more in control) and lowers the level of conflict in the home.

3) Watch out for questions: There are two kinds of questions we never respond to (a) questions to which our children already know the answers, (b) questions they don't need to know the answers to. Answering questions the child already knows tells the child you think he is dumb, or you, the parent, are dumb. Answering questions she doesn't need to know says to the child that you think she's right not to trust you. There is no more powerful message than no response at all.

4) Do not argue with a nonsensical child: Arguing creates chaos and the child may be using it as a way to relieve guilt or anxiety; just getting you to argue with him makes him think he's won. To prevent a sugar overdose effect, think of your words as his reward, and mete them out carefully. Make directives clear, short, and pleasant. If I give my child a direction and he argues with me, I repeat it and say, "Yes Mom" prompting him to repeat. If he continues to argue, I say, "I'm so glad you are still talking at me because I have a lot of chores that need doing." Save your words for more fun interactions such as reading a book together, coaching, or talking about life.

5) The "Lecture Myth:" Parents explain their decisions and lecture their children because they believe that if they find just the right words, and say them in just the right way, or enough times, a light bulb will go off. The children will have a V-8 moment, and suddenly agree that the parents were right all along. They may even thank the parents for their wisdom. In most cases, this is a highly

unlikely occurrence. You will typically only succeed in exhausting yourself and forcing your child into shutdown mode. We do lecture, but we try to reserve our lectures for once-a-month family meetings. And, we lecture not because we think it will change our children, but because we retain a tiny bit of hope that perhaps they will eventually take something we say to heart.

6) Be careful showing disappointment. Parental disappointment is a natural reaction to a child's bad behavior, and it can be a very effective parenting tool. I conducted a study years ago in which I asked college students to write their most positive and negative memories of each of their parents. One of the most popular negative memories was how they disappointed their parents because they had acted badly. These young adults recalled feeling remorse and sadness over disappointing their parents and recalled that this parental reaction was a good deterrent to committing other bad acts. However, parental disappointment induces feelings of shame in children, a feeling traumatized children will fend off with fervor. Therefore, the use of disappointment could have the opposite effect on your children. Additionally, traumatized children often want others to feel as disappointed as they feel and may thrive on making you feel bad. Instead of saying to the child, "I am so disappointed in your behavior," say, "You must feel very disappointed in your behavior. Don't worry, I still love you." Better still, use the coaching method and say...

> Parent/Coach: "This is where you say to me, Mom/ Coach I really messed up and I don't know how to fix it." "Go."

After child repeats back:

> Parent/Coach: "This is where you say to me, Mom Coach, can you help me figure out what to do?" "Go."

After child repeats back:

> Parent/Coach: "Yes, I can. I am so glad you asked me."

7) Find one strength: Intellectual curiosity and gratification in completing tasks are strengths often lacking in traumatized children. However, all children have at least one thing they can do well at some point during their childhoods. Unfortunately, it sometimes takes Olympian efforts to find that one thing. Parents need to provide children with many opportunities to try different things if they hope to find that one thing at which the child can succeed. And when I say succeed, I'm not talking about the common overindulgent trend of parents to spare no amount of money or time finding that one thing that their child not only does well but is a genius at and that ensures his future and world fame. Instead, I'm talking about very simple skills that can be accessed readily.

For example, one of my children, a quitter by nature (or poor nurturing as the case may be), became interested in jogging after I strongly encouraged him to join me. Low and behold, he was good at it. He began running in races and feeling quite proud of himself. He however did not maintain this activity when I did not schedule it. We encourage all our children to get involved with non-competitive sports activities (as opposed to team sports), and group activities such as Aikido, dance, and drama club. At home we encourage model building, jigsaw puzzles, science experiments, and cooking, to name a few.

Never completely remove from the child the privilege of participating in that one special activity. If the child is misbehaving during the activity, tell him he can try again later, or have the teacher or coach "bench" him. If the child is hassling you, you can refuse to drive him to the activity (unless he pays you) and he is more than welcome to find another ride to his activity, but you aren't going to say he can't go.

8) Don't let them use you. Many parents tell me they feel used by their traumatized children, but they can't explain exactly how or why. I suggest that what they are feeling is what is missing -- the giving-back in the relationship (reciprocity). Many traumatized children don't know what to do with parents, so they use them as servants and as an audience. Rygaard's (1998) explanation, from a psychoanalytic perspective, is that these children are arrested at the oral stage of development (infancy) and have an oral fixation; they eat you up and spit you out. When my children make demands on me, I sometimes ask them, "What's in it for me?" to remind them that we are in this relationship together, and I expect them to give back. Initially, this can be in the form of chores. Later, however, you should expect hugs, kisses and thoughtfulness. These are all coachable behaviors.

9) Have fun: This too shall pass. But if you don't have a good sense of humor and lots of playtime with your children, it will pass like molasses through a sieve. Do the unexpected or spontaneous, like jumping in the car and going to a dollar movie in the middle of the day, go bowling, have a picnic on the living room floor. Don't worry if they don't deserve special treats - you do! We are also very cautious sharing information about fun activities

or vacations because our children will get very hyper prior to the event and some of them will show us their worst behaviors just to prove they are not worthy of fun. Sometimes we pack their bags in secret and wake them up the next day, telling them to get into the car without a clue as to where we are going. It's bad enough to think they may pay us back upon our return (no good deed goes unpunished), we don't need to be punished beforehand as well.

10) Do what is in your best interest first: This is such an antithetical practice to what comes naturally for good mommies and daddies. Conventional wisdom dictates that we should sacrifice for our children. However, this is under the assumption that the child will benefit from our sacrifices and will complementarily reciprocate. But some traumatized children are like "Borgs" (a Star Trek analogy). Nothing makes them happy except to assimilate you. If you attempt to make them happy, they may turn around and bite you in the butt. Therefore, if you have a big outing planned, for example, and you suspect that one of your children will make the trip so uncomfortable no one is bound to have a good time, that child must stay home with a sitter. Your child's bad behaviors are not your burden. They are his. You will find that choosing what is in your best interest will ultimately be in your child's best interest.

11) Take care of yourself: I advised a mother who was feeling quite overwhelmed by her insatiable traumatized child to spend some extra time with her birth child with whom she found great satisfaction. She said "That doesn't seem fair to my foster child. He's been through so much. I've been trying to treat them equally." No doubt, the traumatized child needs copious amounts of parent time. However, parents need to stay emotionally

filled up and energized to cope with and help a traumatized child. There is no better way than spending time with those who love you.

Along these same lines, don't start some new parenting technique when you are tired, angry with the child, or stressed from other life events. You will only exasperate an already difficult situation and won't know for sure if the technique is truly worthwhile or not.

12) Do not attempt to be the child's friend (unless you have given up on being her parent or coach). This is a mistake many foster and adoptive parents make because they feel sorry for the child and for what she has been through. The last person a traumatized child is going to feel safe with, and attach to, is someone she views as weaker, dumber, and less in control of himself than she is; only adults who are superior to her can protect her. All children need parents who are effective and emotionally competent -- traumatized children need parents who are exceptionally effective and emotionally competent.

13) Don't push too hard: If you are overly anxious to fix the child and too needy for affection from the child, you will in fact thwart your long-term efforts. As Bettelheim said over fifty years ago, the parent-child relationship is the most complex of all relationships. "...the difficulties of almost all emotionally disturbed children originated in the relationship to a parent. It is therefore unrealistic to expect them to be able to form successful relationships to parent substitutes after so short a time. But since no other types of relationships are available, the child depends for satisfaction of his needs on conformity with the established pattern. He recognizes what is useful to him and pretends a child-parent relationship. The result is a pseudo-relationship, which rules out any later formation of a true

one… Immediate loving or mothering of a child implies obligation to return such love, a response which is beyond the disturbed child's emotional capacity at first and results only in feelings of worthlessness and guilt." Therefore, if you push too hard and give too much, traumatized children will seek your conveniences as opposed to your love (Bettleheim, pg 17-18, 1950).

14) Feeling loved is on them. Many traumatized children want to feel loved but they can't because they don't love. My children all believe that my youngest child is my favorite and that I love her the most. The fact is, I love all my children and treat them in loving ways. The difference between my youngest child and my other children is that my youngest loves me the most. Therefore, undoubtedly, she feels loved the most. I tell my children that loving them is easy, them loving me is the hard part. And that's on them!

15) Stop trying to out-think them. You cannot think like a traumatized child, and perhaps learning how would not be in your best interest. But remember, they cannot think like you either, which means you have the advantage. Use it wisely!

16) Be careful discussing your child's behaviors with your friends and family. I'm not sure that all of my family members believe me yet, and I have a Ph.D. in developmental psychology and wrote a book on the subject. Instead, talk to those who better understand what you're experiencing, such as other foster and adoptive parents, your social worker, and experts in the field. Support groups can be very helpful in providing opportunities to vent as well as resources for respite. However, should you slip and share your experiences with those who "don't get it," you can use my pat answer to "All kids do that." I say, "Yes, they do, but not ten times a day, every day, for years on

end." Also, if they suggest that their birth children's behaviors compare to my traumatized children's behaviors in intensity, frequency, and duration, I have a good therapist's phone number handy. (I'm always stupefied when parents want to compare their children's behaviors to my children's behaviors as if we're swapping recipes. But I do understand that it is their way of trying to make sense out of something completely foreign and unfathomable).

Another good tactic is to ask the other person what they receive in their relationships with their children. In other words, what makes them happy satisfied or proud to be a parent. As they begin to rattle off things like, "My child shows me he loves me in so many ways, "or "My child gives me hugs and kisses every night," or "My child is so much fun to be around," you can say, "My child doesn't do that." You'll be pleasantly surprised at their concerned responses ; talking about the positive behaviors your children do not perform seems to elicit more empathy than talking about the negative behaviors they do perform.

17) We strive to create a simple, structured, protective environment for our children. (A well-meaning relative once asked me, "Aren't you being overprotective? How will they ever get along in the real world?" To which I replied, "I think my children have seen enough of the real world"). We've home schooled all of our children for periods of time, which allows us to structure their days, based on their individual needs. Home schooling also allows us to (1) reduce conflict by restricting the number of people in our children's lives, (2) minimize their opportunities for acting inauthentically or manipulatively, and (3) provide more "mommy and daddy" or "coach" time which increases attachment opportunities.

Our approach to home schooling is that the children are responsible for their own education. We are responsible for providing the time, structure, and materials. We do not battle over schoolwork. If one of our children wants to sit in his room and read Garfield comics all morning, he will pay the natural consequence for that choice. On the other hand, we do build-in incentives for completing work, like computer time (but not the internet), playtime with Mom or Dad, and helping Mom and Dad with household projects. One of our children is significantly learning disabled so we have placed academic performance on a back burner for him. Instead he helps out more around the house and is beginning to learn the construction trade.

We emphasize physical and emotional health in addition to academic performance. We encourage daily exercise (e.g., jogging, swimming, calisthenics, hiking, boxing), and those of our children who are coachable (in the traditional sense of the word) participate in additional physical activities (sports teams, dance, gymnastics, etc.). We also emphasize personal achievement as opposed to competition, although we must say that boxing has helped build the confidence of one of our sons like nothing we have tried in the past.

We revisit their abuse histories often and challenge faulty thinking and behaviors with "Love and Logic." We steer their interactions into prosocial avenues and offer interpretations of behaviors and feelings that may be blocking enjoyment of, or participation in, an activity. We eat a healthy diet with lots of fresh food, and limit sweets and snacking, which helps build self-control. We watch little TV, and it is always supervised. Our home is neat, clean, spacious, quiet, and kid friendly. The children have a few regularly assigned chores but mostly they are expected to do chores as we deem necessary at any given time. The children know that at age eighteen, if they want to continue living with us, they must have a full time job and/or be in school, and act respectful, responsible, and fun to be around.

As parents we must play "traffic cop" much of the time, dividing and conquering, insuring 24/7 supervision, and directing most of their activities. In between, we love (our lovable children), coach, nurture, and educate our children, and explain to friends and loved ones why our family has to function differently from theirs. We also take good care of our marriage and ourselves by placing both above all else; we are definitely the King and Queen of our home.

We reserve quiet alone times for ourselves, both separately and together. We make time for intimacy and sex (sometimes both at the same time!). And we even get away on vacation by ourselves once a year. We are careful to support each other in parenting issues and save challenges for private discussions. We facilitate regular family meetings with our children to let them know of their progress and what needs improving. Although we stick with the above stated plan pretty consistently, about 20% of the time we lose it, get very angry, and say and do stupid things.

18) End result. In spite of the doom and gloom presented in this book, traumatized children can improve over time, some internally and externally, some only externally. At this writing, two of our four children are functioning beautifully, in spite of some horrific abuse histories. They didn't start out this way, but through consistent parenting, a well-designed, controlled environment, and therapeutic interventions they have come

through the trauma, bought-in to the parent-child relationship, and appear quite normal; they have internalized the meaning of "family." Of these two, one child is vulnerable to relapses because the abuse was so extensive and long-lasting (the first eight years of life). But this child has a deep desire to be healthy and to live a normal life, and trusts us to guide that process (most of the time).

The other two children function well as long as we are supervising and directing them. However, if we turn our backs, they quickly revert to old anti-family and immature behaviors and attitudes. In other words, they depend on us to externally control them because they have not yet internalized our love or our home environment, in spite of having the same opportunities as the other two children. Some people (professional and lay) predicted that one of these two children would never function in a home, but for the time being we are beating those odds, and without medication!

However, we are concerned about their futures, one because of narcissistic tendencies and the other because of poor academic abilities and performance, and lack of motivation. But we are working hard to come up with alternative lines of work for the latter. We believe there are many avenues for reaching what ever potential is left and we feel a sense of responsibility to teach them some skill they can take with them when they leave the nest, whether they choose to use it or not.

Our children vary in temperaments, strengths and weaknesses, and level and type of trauma exposure, which explains why the different outcomes. Unfortunately, no pattern has yet been identified, through research or otherwise, that would tell us how to predict which child will fare well and which will not.

Advise To Yet-To-Be Birth Parents

There is a literature base that promotes "Attachment Parenting" from which much of the practices of developmental reparenting stems. Those who use attachment-parenting techniques say it hones/trains parental intuition and attunement skills. When parents are attuned to their infants they respect the child's individual temperament, and make themselves aware of the child's "cuing" behaviors; a responsive parent and a cue-giving child bring out the best in both. On the other hand, detachment parenting (restrained) causes both baby and parent to not trust each other and to become insensitive to one another. The fussy or difficult baby is in most need of attachment parenting. There are several web sites on the Internet from which I learned about attachment parenting practices by typing "attachment parenting" into the search engine. Attachment Parenting Practices include:

1) a commitment to the baby and to the marriage (stable and fulfilled)

2) spending time preparing your parenting style rather than the baby's room

3) breast feeding that attends to the baby's signs of needing food and comfort rather than watching the clock or ounces.

4) weaning - "to ripen" child directed "I am filled with this relationship and ready to move on to another." When infants/children are weaned according to your timetable instead of theirs they are prone to anger, aggression, and moodiness.

5) prompt responses to crying

6) openness to various sleeping arrangements (e.g., bed next to parent bed, family bed)

7) traveling as Mother-Baby or Father-Baby unit (marsupial parenting: "wearing" the baby)

Parents who use attachment parenting say the payoff is immense: parents know their children better, are more confidant in their parenting, have more realistic expectations of their children and of themselves, and have more harmonious family relationships. They say their children are a source of joy rather than aggravation. The children reared with this method tend to be compliant and caring, have high self-esteem, are better behaved (trust is the basis for giving someone authority), have a better sense of right and wrong, and a healthy conscience (guilt). Parents and experts say this method helps children feel right and, therefore, they are more likely to act right, to internalize values, to have full access to emotions, to have more intimate relationships (attached to people not things), to have nurturing qualities (sensitive to needs of others), and to make better future parents and mates.

"It's a good thing to give a baby and young child physical contact, especially when they want it and seek it. It doesn't spoil them. It doesn't make them clingy. It doesn't make them addicted to being held. Warm, sensitive care does not create dependency; it liberates, and enables autonomy." Mary Ainsworth

One word of caution however, do not confuse your child's wants with needs. While it is true that you can never spoil an infant, it is quite easy to spoil a toddler and older children. And many parents who had the best intentions with attachment parenting in infancy fail to adjust their parenting to the needs of the child. Check to be sure you are not giving in to the child's every whim, confusing overindulgence with nurturing, making the child the highest priority (over marital needs), being a friend instead of a parent, or giving too much stuff and too much permission too soon. Overindulgent parenting results in many of the same negative child outcomes as neglectful parenting, because overindulgence is neglecting what children truly need.

One more note:

Please be aware of political forces aimed at keeping parents apart from their children. It's amazing the lengths that some in this country will go to in steering parents away from staying home with their children the first three years of life. For example, legislation promotes and financially supports subsidized day care, back to work efforts, and early childhood education (out of the home), all of which limit parental choice. While there is no doubt early childhood education is effective in helping disadvantaged children in getting a leg up on school, the data do not support the pervasive belief that all children must receive early childhood education to be more successful in school and better socialized. That is a complete perversion of the data promoted to benefit the country's economic state; early childhood "education" provides paraprofessionals with work, and gets parents back to their jobs sooner.

In other words, preschools and day cares are good for business, but they are not necessarily good for families. The sad news is that this policy does not respect the significance of the infant-parent relationship as the catalyst for emotional and social health and, yes, academic performance. With policies like these we are ensured never to reach our potential as individuals, couples, or a society.

Suggested Readings

"Parenting With Love and Logic"
by Foster Cline & Jim Fay

"When Love Is Not Enough"
by Nancy Thomas

"Therapeutic Parenting: It's A Matter Of Attitude"
by Debra Hague

"Parenting The Hurt Child"
by Greg Keck & Regina Kupecky

ASSESSMENT and TREATMENT

I wrote this book to explain why, from developmental and relationship perspectives, traumatized children think, feel, and act the way they do, to shed light on the unique family dynamics of adoptive homes, and to provide some new ways that parents can help both themselves and their children. But where does therapy fit into all of this? Many traumatized children will participate in a variety of therapeutic interventions – a few will be effective, most will not. So that both parents and professionals can be better informed consumers of these interventions, I have included a brief outline on assessment and treatment protocols that can be found fleshed out in many other books on the subject (see references).

Assessment

One of the most important elements needed in working with traumatized children is a thorough assessment and/or evaluation of the child's condition. An assessment estimates the significance of the child's condition while an evaluation expresses significance in terms of numbers and statistics. A trained professional should complete both assessments and evaluations. If the person completing the assessment is not also the therapist he or she will usually make referrals to specific professionals or therapists based on the results of the assessment.

The following is a brief outline of what can be assessed and/or evaluated and what instruments are appropriate. This is not an exhaustive list, and there may be many other instruments available for conducting good assessments and/or evaluations. Then too, I am not a clinician, so these suggestions are not based on my experience, but rather on my understanding of the literature.

For more information on assessments and evaluations see *Help For the Hopeless Child* by Ronald Federici (1998).

The first three assessments plus at least one psychological evaluation and one neurological evaluation, are absolute necessities. Developmental evaluations are discretionary, but van Gulden's method of assessing object-relations is very helpful in informing treatment. All co-morbid conditions should be identified and then prioritized. For example, if a child is diagnosed with RAD and ADHD, it is likely the RAD is the primary problem and it should be treated aggressively, perhaps prior to drug therapy for ADHD.

1) History: birth through current age including attachment disruptions and current level of child's functioning (e.g., behavioral, cognitive, emotional, social, physical, moral, and birth parent demographics)
2) Observations of child in natural settings (school, day care, home)
3) Interviews with all people who know the child (e.g., parents, teachers, coaches, therapists, social workers past and present)
4) Psychological evaluation (Randolph, 2002)
    a. Randolph Attachment Disorder Questionnaire (RADQ)
    b. Rorschach Ink Blot Test
    c. Revised Dimensions of Temperament Scale (RDTS)
    d. Millon Adolescent Personality Inventory

(MAPI)

e. Personality Inventory for Children (PIC)

f. Child Behavior Checklist (CBC)

5) Neurological impairment/immaturity evaluation

    a. developmental movements and cross crawl abilities (Randolph, 2002)

    b. Quantitative Electroencephalogram (QEEG; neuropsychological): brain imaging in which brain waves are processed and analyzed statistically, then mapped by amplitude and frequency.

    c. Bender-Gestalt

    d. Trails Test

6) Developmental evaluation

    a. learning and motor skills

    b. object-relations (van Gulden & Riedel, 2000).

7) Co-morbid disorders (differential diagnoses)

    a. Revised Children's Manifest Anxiety Scale

    b. Rorschach Ink Blot Test

    c. Occupational Evaluation (Sensory Integration Disorder)

    d. Beech Brook Attachment Disorder Diagnostic Questionnaire

8) Parent evaluation

    a. Millon Clinical Multiaxial Inventory

    b. parenting history

    c. in-home observation

Therapeutic Protocols

Treatment for traumatized children does not always entail help from a therapist. However, to go it alone is risky and lonely. Although parents have the major role in fostering the emotional health of their traumatized children, the therapist acts as a change agent for the child and helps to drive the child to new levels of understanding and acceptance. In addition, therapists can provide tremendous support to the parents who often feel abused by their child; living with a traumatized child often evokes a parent's most negative defense mechanisms that often parallel those of the child (e.g., projection, splitting, denial, hopelessness, guilt; Rygaard, 1998).

Therapists vary in academic and professional experiences. There are mental health practitioners, private practice psychotherapists, social workers, psychologists and psychiatrists. Some specialize in child therapies and others in family therapies. Often times there is confusion amongst these professionals as to what each of them can offer, should offer, and do offer. For example, some practitioners who work with attachment-disordered children are referred to as "attachment" therapists, but this is misleading. Most of these therapists were first trained in general theories and methods, and then received several additional years of training to work with traumatized children. Their therapy focuses on remediating the effects of early childhood trauma on childhood developmental tasks, including that of attachment.

In choosing a therapist several considerations should be made related to the therapist's philosophical beliefs, theoretical approaches, and technical practices. These form the underlying foundation of the therapist's work and will require parental buy-in if the child is to fully

benefit. Unfortunately, at this time, to the best of my knowledge, there is no comprehensive research or reference material that explains cohesively and thoroughly all of the philosophical beliefs, theoretical perspectives, and technical practices employed in current therapeutic work with traumatized children. As a result, there is much discordance in the psychological community as to what is good, ethical, and effective practice in
treating traumatized children. And while the psychological community is short on research and knowledge in this area, there is no shortage on professional opinion.

Philosophical Beliefs

Philosophical beliefs are universal ideas regarding human nature that cannot necessarily be proven or dis-proven. For example one therapist may believe that all or most children are fragile, tell the truth, and are trusting, while another therapist believes that all or most children are resilient, lie, and are mistrustful. One therapist may hold the belief that infants are born as a clean slate on which environmental experiences will write their future, while another holds the belief that most children's live will be determined by their genetic makeup.

One profound philosophical difference between traditional play therapists and therapists who specialize in working with traumatized children is the issue of trust. The former believe it is their job to help the traumatized child trust the therapist before they can work on the child's issues and thus spend a considerable amount of time in therapy working towards that end. The latter assume that these children are incapable of trust (initially) and therefore do not expect them to transfer in the therapy session a relationship of which they have never experienced: a child cannot give that which she does not possess (Bettelheim,

1950). They also believe that traumatized children build phony rapports with adults and, therefore, the therapists do not concern themselves with relationship building as a precursor to therapeutic work.

Instead, rapport and trust are built through immediate, honest, forthright validation of the child's trauma history and current behavior issues. Sometimes this means saying to the child that her parents were inadequate, that people hurt her and they were wrong, that the therapist understands why she doesn't trust anyone, and that her current behaviors are not going to get her what she really wants or that which is good for her. This approach is effective in several ways, all of which encourage the child to make changes. First, when the child "knows" that the therapist "knows," she doesn't spend a lot of emotional energy trying to hide or deny her past. Second, identifying and challenging the child's defenses (e.g., charm, distraction, flirting) frustrates the child, but helps her move through the therapy more quickly.

Third, the child will immediately feel a sense of security, and dread that her therapist is not going to tiptoe around her. These confrontive tactics, though powerful, can alienate a child. Some traumatized children are not always happy to visit their therapists, and sometimes say they don't like their therapists. However, therapists using the above stated approach wouldn't expect their clients to be happy working through their trauma, or to like the therapist -- until they are emotionally healthy.

Some foster/adoptive parents, social workers, and even some mental health professionals believe adults should not broach the subject of abuse or tell traumatized children the truth of their pasts (another philosophical belief). But, that makes me wonder, "Who are we kidding?

The child lived it." When adults whitewash, sugarcoat, deny, or fear a child's trauma they minimize or nullify the child's life experiences, which can retraumatize the child. What's worse these "helping" adults may appear to the child complicit in the abuse. Furthermore, without validation from healthy adults, children will be less likely to face, accept, and heal from their trauma history. As stated in the section of parent-child relationships, honesty and certainty breed a sense of security and control. Therefore, a relationship, no matter how tenuous to begin with, can be built stronger and more quickly if it starts with all the cards on the table.

Theoretical Approaches

There are specific theoretical approaches most often used in therapy with children, although it is beyond the scope of this book to detail any one of them, as they are quite extensive. Full descriptions can be found in many texts on the theory and practice of psychotherapy. One of my favorite authors on the subject is Gerald Corey. Examples of theoretical approaches are:

- Psychodynamic (thought-oriented; change thinking and behavior will follow)
    i. Analytic
    ii. Psychosocial
    iii. Object-relations
- Behavioral (action-oriented; change behavior and thinking will follow)
- Cognitive Behavioral (behavior and thought work together to create change)
- Family Systems (child is best understood and assisted within the family context)

- Reality (responsibility for thought and behavior lies within the individual)

Therapeutic Techniques

Within each of these philosophical beliefs and theoretical approaches certain therapeutic techniques are employed. Therapists may share similar beliefs and approaches and employ different techniques, or they may share different beliefs and approaches and employ similar techniques. For example, one therapist trained in psychodynamic theory may use play therapy as her primary mode of therapeutic intervention, whereas another may use Theraplay or cognitive restructuring as his primary modes of therapeutic intervention. Many therapists, although trained in certain theoretical camps, are quite eclectic in the techniques they employ, meaning they will use a variety of techniques and adjust these techniques, within their philosophical and theoretical frameworks, and depending on the needs and receptivity of the client. Some of these techniques are:

- EMDR - eye movement desensitization reprogramming
- psycho-drama - act out both negative and positive interactions to regain power; reenact traumatic episodes with alternative dialogues and outcomes
- cognitive restructuring - confront thinking errors and reorganize thoughts
- narrative story telling - give the child new and positive birth and toddler-hood histories
- play - dolls and other play objects encourage free association of negative experiences
- dialectic - problem solving focus, analyze function of behaviors

- paradoxical - client is encouraged to do the opposite of what he should be doing to lessen desire or diminish the thrill (ex. a child who curses to be aggressive is allowed designated cursing times)
- behavior modification - practice or "try-out" new behaviors
- somatic- body movement to access preverbal areas of the brain and memory
- massage - overcome fear of touch or sensory integration problems; done with clothes on
- relaxation - breathing, yoga
- flooding - exaggeration of emotions or behaviors
- re-enactment - to relieve a repressed emotion
- Theraplay - a nonverbal and physically stimulating technique that encourages physical closeness, and compliance to parental controls and directions
- regression - recapture the steps and stages of early attachment experiences; draw awareness of child dependency on parent; encourage trust that parent can and will take care of child's needs
- hypnosis - recover repressed memory or suggest alternate ego messages
- neuro-feedback - stimulate neural pathway and synaptic formation, slow down or speed up brain activity, promote receptivity to therapeutic interventions.
- Sensory-motor integration - physical therapy that increases appropriate interpretations of sensory input

Controversial Techniques

Two of the more controversial techniques in therapeutic work with traumatized children are "holding" and "regression." Holding is often referred to as a therapy, but in fact it is a technique and is often incorporated into a treatment plan that includes many of the other techniques stated above. The idea of holding is not new to therapeutic interventions. It is a long-standing assumption that a therapist psychologically "holds" the client by providing a safe and nurturing environment that is consistent, and that encourages and affirms the client's sense of wholeness (see Winnecott, 1965-1989). Holding is also not new in terms of parent-child relationships. Parents hold their children to nurture them and to control them, and in so doing provide undivided attention, empathy, protection, and care that reassures the infant/child in an ever changing world and self. What is new about holding, in the therapeutic sense, is the blending of psychological holding with the physical holding that naturally occurs in the parent-child relationship.

James (1994) describes inappropriate coercive holding as that which restrains the child for other than protective reasons, stimulates by poking, prodding, tickling, tapping, or moving parts of the body, and interferes with body functions by covering eyes or inhibiting breathing. James is referring to techniques also known as "rage reduction therapy." The goal of this therapy is to provoke a high level of arousal in the child in hopes he will release the repressed rage that is interfering in his attaching to caregivers.

Rage-reduction therapy was derived in part from learning theory. According to John Watson, the founding father of learning theory, there are only three innate emotions: fear, rage, and love. He suggested that rage is elicited by the restriction of bodily movements. Therefore, it was assumed that because traumatized children are filled with rage from unrequited needs, provoking rage by holding the child against his will should free the child to love again. Some therapists still use this method, but it is not a popular method. Other therapists use a method that entails holding a raging child (or adult) after the child has became evoked from something in the therapy. The therapist is sometimes unsure of what might bring on such a rage for a particular client, and is caught unaware and must contain the client.

When a known person restricts a non-traumatized child's bodily movement, the child feels rage, but not fear. However, when a known person restricts a traumatized child's bodily movement, the child feels rage and fear. Fear mediates flight. But the fear may be a paratactic distortion, so the therapist must hold the child to assure the child he has nothing to fear from her and no need to run away. Therefore, what seems intuitive - don't hold a traumatized child against his will, is actually counterintuitive - you need to hold a traumatized child who is raging or he will go on believing he has something to fear. Holding an angry child also tells him that he is safe and the adults can control him (protect him) when he cannot control himself. And the holding may induce a bonding event that can enhance attachment.

Although the therapeutic techniques James describes sound offensive, particularly when perpetrated on a child who was traumatized, most of them can be explained within the context and purpose of the treatment plan. For example, tapping (EMDR) and moving the body (somatic therapy) are accepted techniques in relieving symptoms of PTSD and for processing preverbal memories. Usually the therapist incorporates EMDR with story telling while the caregiver is holding the child in a loving non-coercive manner. Somatic work is often done in the form of games, and rough and tumble play with the therapist or parent. And it is also used while holding the child to identify and release stored trauma in the body. Many practitioners are beginning to incorporate massage (clothes on) into their therapeutic plans for the same reason.

Interestingly, many professionals and society at large don't seem to mind parents "holding" their children to control them and condone "holding" children with medication and lock down facilities. Yet, they believe physically "holding" a child for therapeutic purposes, even when the child doesn't seem to mind and even enjoys it, is offensive and violates his human rights.

Three of my children have been involved in therapy with trauma specialists with varying degrees of success. The therapists, my husband, and I have practiced holding techniques with these three children and rarely were the techniques used against their will. On the contrary, they enjoyed being held (much more so during the therapy than at other times). It was actually during this therapy that one of my children revealed his sexual abuse history. Some practitioners may be alarmed by this declaration, assuming that holding a child may cause him to make false allegations of abuse. However, in our case, the abuse was real and appeared only to be revealed because of this therapeutic process; it was never revealed during the three years we had already lived with this child. Because talk and play therapies are less confrontive, they may be less successful in creating the type of change, conducive atmosphere often needed by traumatized children.

I have observed other families in therapy with trauma specialists and have been impressed by some of the results. Some of these therapists do not hold the child, but encourage the parents to hold the child, and some use no holding techniques at all. Although I know there is still much to learn regarding therapeutic interventions with traumatized children, I am convinced that traditional play or talk therapy alone is not an effective treatment course for most of these children. On the other hand, I am equally convinced that a severely traumatized child who is diagnosed with attachment disorder may move up the continuum of attachment, but will likely never become a securely attached child, no matter what interventions are implemented.

Regression
Another controversial technique is called "regression." Regression can be conducted in several ways: with a therapist via hypnosis, with a therapist via transference, with the caregiver via immersion. Regression via hypnosis is usually done for the purpose of recovering repressed memories and is the most controversial because false memories can be prompted by the therapist's suggestions. Regression via transference helps clients rework negative parent-child experiences by transferring their negative feelings on to an accepting surrogate parent (i.e., the therapist). Regression via immersion involves the reenactment of developmental steps missed in early childhood, with the current parent.

Regression is controversial because some people believe it is not possible to recapture early childhood experiences or to rework these experiences with more positive outcomes. However, regarding treatment for traumatized children, particularly if the child is young (age six or under), regression immersion can be a very successful technique and can be performed by parents with time, energy, willingness and some guidance from a professional.

Immersion allows the toddler or young child to be the "baby" once again, and in so doing relearn (or in some cases learn for the first time) the joy and freedom of being completely dependent on a responsive, nurturing, consistent caregiver. A regression immersion treatment plan entails parents providing complete and continuous care-taking activities such as:

a. feeding with eye contact
b. touch, massage, snuggling
c. movement, dancing, tossing
d. story telling, baby games
e sleeping together
f. carrying (parents only)
g. bottles and pacifiers
h. diapers
i. comforting by parents only
j holding in cradle position

This is difficult for some parents to carry out if they have maturity demands for toddlers and young children. We regressed our youngest child and enjoyed it immensely because we'd never had the opportunity to care for an infant. She came to us at 2.75 years of age and was exhibiting many disturbing behaviors (e.g., no eye contact, hyper vigilance, over friendliness with strangers, tantrums, aggression, hoarding and stealing food, not holding on when held, pushing away physical contact, noncompliance). Her birth mother was a drug addict and transient who often left her with neighbors for long periods of time. To our knowledge, our daughter was not sexually abused, but she did see her mother having sex.

When she was three years of age, we put in place a regression plan that included all of the above stated elements; she became our baby. The regression lasted three months with periodic follow-ups for about a year. She resisted almost all of our activities for the first month, but then began to relax into this new arrangement. For example, she would not fall asleep with us (sometimes she would keep herself awake until she would drop to the ground and fall asleep with her eyes open). So, we would wait until she fell asleep and then place her in our bed. In the morning she would wake up startled, confused about her surroundings, and uncomfortable with the intimacy (e.g., not laying still, not molding). But we would play and wrestle with her, and after a month she became more comfortable. I remember, clearly, the first time she fell asleep in my arms nearly a year after she was placed with us. I cried, knowing we had made it over the hump. It was one of the happiest days of my life.

I initiated more physical contact with her by playing with shave cream during her bath. To much giggles and suggestions by her I would make a design on her tummy, rub it out, and start anew. Baths sometimes took an hour. Initially she resisted because she wanted to do it herself, but she soon learned if she wanted to play she had to do it Mommy's way. Our bath time ritual also included swaddling her in a towel and holding her like a baby, rubbing good smelling lotions on her body, and brushing her hair and her teeth for her.

Story telling included messages of normal parent-child relationships. Her favorite was about a hippo that runs off to play with her in the woods. Meanwhile, her Mommy is fretting and worrying about her, and when she realizes she forgot to tell her Mommy where she was going, and her Mommy is probably worried, she rushes home to her Mommy's arms, and she, her Mommy, and the hippo all sit down to eat cinnamon toast (her favorite). At meal times we would pretend she was a baby bird being fed by the mommy bird, or we would play airplane, always with eye contact.

We knew it was time to step back from the regression when the concerning behaviors tapered off and she was acting much more comfortable in the relationship, was more compliant, was playing with the bottle instead of drinking out of it, was asking for help, and was seeking proximity and closeness without any ulterior motive. At that point, we allowed more independent behaviors, and used relapses of old behaviors as indicators that she needed us to be more in control.

At the writing of this book our daughter is 7.5 years old and securely attached; she is totally in love with us and feeling good about it (she embraces her love for us as opposed to feeling scared or ambivalent). She is on target developmentally, and although she still has a feisty temper she is a pure delight to be around. She still hops into bed with us every morning, and asks me to feed her foods she doesn't like because, as she puts it, "That's how it gets Mommy love in it to make it taste good."

Some people might think that she was so young when she came to us, she would have become healthy even if we hadn't' regressed her. I can't argue with that thinking. It is true that some of the research on the success of therapeutic interventions suggests that time in and of itself can be good therapy. However, practitioners know of children who experienced trauma and came to loving homes much younger than she, and still never got healthy. I may not know for sure that the regression worked, but it feels like it did. I wish I had done it with a couple of my other children.

Where and When

Aside from the "how" of therapeutic interventions, practitioners also vary on the where and when of their therapeutic interventions. Some practitioners work in offices and some go into the home, some use the traditional fifty minute hour - once a week schedule, while others allow for as much time as is needed for as many days in a row as needed. For example, a front-loading method entails the therapist seeing the client for five to ten consecutive days, 3-4 hours per day. This "intensive" practice is meant to help the client work through difficult experiences (such as childhood abuse, neglect and chaos), and take responsibility for behavior and current relationship status in a condensed, accelerated format with no recuperation time in-between sessions. Often weekly visits of one to two hours a week follow the front-loading. Also, therapists working with traumatized children are likely to provide a continuum of services including: (1) in-home parent coaching, (2) respite care, (3) family counseling, and (4) couples and marriage therapy.

Training of Mental Health Professionals

Foster and adoptive families have access to free mental health services through Medicaid. However, many mental health providers have indicated to their local departments of social services and state adoption agencies several limitations in servicing traumatized children. First, they have little knowledge of how to prioritize for treatment traumatized children's multiple psychological diagnoses (e.g., learning disabilities, ADD/ADHD, sensory integration dysfunction, and bipolar, attachment, post traumatic stress, oppositional defiant, conduct, anxiety, depressive, and personality disorders).

Second, they are all too familiar with treatment models that have proven ineffective in working with the multiple disorders exhibited by traumatized children (e.g., psychodynamic therapy, play therapy, drug therapy). However, they have little knowledge and training in therapeutic models and skills that successfully diminish the myriad antisocial/antifamily behaviors manifested by many foster and adopted children.

Third, their agencies and private practices lack the continuum of services necessary to improve foster and adoptive family functioning. Those private practitioners equipped to provide some or all of the continuum of services stated earlier often do not take Medicaid or insurance and therefore are financially inaccessible to most needy foster/adoptive families. Consequently, state departments of social services and adoption agencies are observing an exacerbation of traumatized children's weaknesses, reluctance on the part of some foster parents to make adoption commitments, increasing numbers of adoption disruptions, and increased placements of children into out-of-home leveled programs (e.g., group homes and residential treatment facilities). These immediate consequences have long term effects for all of society as witnessed by the #1 construction business in the country - the building of prisons.

If we ever hope to catch up with and stem this problem, mental health and private practice professionals, respite providers, and group home facilities around the country need access to on-going, in-depth training on assessments, effects of abuse/neglect/chaos on psycho-social stages of child development and early brain development, family life unique to adoptive homes, empirically based therapeutic philosophies and techniques, and technical assistance on service evaluation methods. Training sessions should provide exposure to newer more successful therapeutic models and access to professionals who specialize in the multiple diagnostic areas most typically associated with abused and neglected children.

The Relationship Coach Model in Therapeutic Practice

Most therapists who work with traumatized children know that a major part of the intervention lies in supporting the parents. In most cases this entails instructing the parents on changing their behaviors, attitudes, etc. in hopes that the child will respond (change). But the child is not being asked to do anything positive for the parent. On the contrary, many times the child is asked to stop taking action and the parents are instructed on how to implement consequences for every infraction of the family rules. This becomes infuriating for many parents who have tried so many different parenting practices to manage their child and must continue to do all the work because the child has not internalized prosocial behaviors and attitudes.

Many of these parents feel tremendous guilt over not being able to help these children, and for no longer loving them and even hating them. It is unacceptable to their nature to not want to care for and love a child who is so obviously hurt and damaged. It is important for the parents and the therapists of traumatized children to realize two facts: (1) these parents are living in domestic violence situations, so negative feelings are absolutely natural, healthy, and acceptable, (2) stopping bad behaviors does not guarantee the onset of good behaviors.

The Relationship Coach Model resolves these issues in two ways. First, because the child is expected (and coached) to use positive emotional engagement behaviors with the parent/coach before receiving positive emotional engagement behaviors from the parent/coach, the parent/coach is less likely to feel overburdened and overwhelmed by expectations of their own performance, as well as under whelmed and disappointed by the child's lack of reciprocity. As a result, parental guilt is relieved and the parents may be more likely to continue their efforts. Second, the positive behavior survey tool can be used by the therapist to focus the child on what she is supposed to be doing as opposed to what she is not supposed to be doing, and to give concrete instructions to children and parents on what children are to give back in the relationship.

One Woman's Story

In conducting an observation of a foster child at his school I interviewed his teacher regarding her perceptions of the child. She was keenly aware of his subtle but odd behaviors and the repercussions for this child if he didn't get help. I asked her how she knew so much and she relayed the following story to me, which she later gave me permission to use in this book.

"I was shot five times by my ex-husband. We had been separated for a couple of years and he was coming to visit our teenage son. He walked in the door and shot me once in my neck, twice in my side, once in my arm, and once in my leg. The doctors didn't expect me to survive, but I fooled them. At the trial, my ex-husband claimed he had been insane at the time of the shooting and that he was very sorry. But when the jury found him guilty he swore he would hunt me down and kill me. "You see, I was already a victim of what you are trying to avoid with him." (as she pointed to the child I was there to observe).

My husband was a chameleon, and his whole life was a lie. His parents were wonderful, but he didn't think so. They said he was a really difficult child. They said he was mean, always running the show, wouldn't listen or do what his parents wanted of him. I never saw any of that until after we were married. He was sooo charming -- charming as a snake. Just prior to the shooting he was fired from his job because they figured out he had faked his college degree and job histories. I think all of his lies were catching up to him and he had nobody to blame but me -- he always blamed me for everything. I thought if I just did this or that he would be happy, but he never was. And he would never take 'no' for an answer, if you know what I mean. He just thought he should have what ever he wanted and if you said 'no' he would take it or do it anyway. But he wouldn't believe anything anyone told him, least of all me. If I said it was raining outside, he'd have to go check it out for himself. Now he says he was depressed and that's why he did all of the things he did. I'm not scared of him anymore, I just feel sorry for him. You know, he was adopted when he was just a year old."

Afterward

There are many people who share the sentiment that no child should be considered unadoptable. I'm sorry, but someone has to say it -- not every child is adoptable. Or maybe a better way of saying it is that every child is adoptable, but not all adopted children can live in a family. It's been cited that some very famous, seemingly well-adjusted, successful people were adopted. However most of the famous people often mentioned as being adopted were adopted as newborns. Unfortunately, of the 50,000 American children waiting to be adopted, few are newborns. Many are hard to place due to ethnicity, sibling status, and disabilities. The greatest deterrent to being adopted is age; the average age of a child in foster care is 10. But age in and of itself is not really the problem. Older foster children are not difficult to place because they are older. They are difficult to place because the abuse, neglect, or chaos experienced before their tenure with social services makes them extremely difficult to live with.

As some of us know from experience, and what we have learned from all of the current research on early brain development, exposure to trauma during the first three years of life can cause irreparable brain damage manifesting in social, emotional, and cognitive dysfunction. The most damaging seems to be a lack of trust in other human beings: the first developmental task and the fundamental building block of all current and future relationships, and potential learning.

When children don't trust they won't let you parent them. They do not take direction, heed advice, or interpret limit setting and support as safety and love; they don't buy into the reciprocal nature of the parent-child relationship --

parents provide unconditional love and security and children respond with adoration and compliance. In addition, many of these children will not live up to their cognitive or physical potential because they're not coachable. They will sabotage adults' efforts, play stupid and fake ailments; losing is not relevant to them as long as they control the game. They will fight for control over the most mundane issues with subtlety, cunning, and aggression. Fantasy, immaturity, and self and other-destruction are a way of life for them. Contrary to popular belief, love is not enough to repair the damage.

Early childhood experiences become hardwired in the brain -- good or bad, the brain is an equal opportunity learner. Children who experienced trauma during those years go on to live like POW's, acting as if they are still in the war zone even though they now live in loving, safe environments. To sum it up, they don't function well in or out of families (a significant number of prisoners, mental institution patients, and homeless people were foster/adopted children).

No young child who experiences trauma escapes without some kind of damage, and for us to market them as normal children waiting for a loving home, is unfair to them and to good-hearted but unsuspecting parents. Furthermore, this approach implies that a loving home provided at some future point during childhood can repair the damage wrought in infancy, which in turn nullifies the significance of the birth parent-child relationship. The former is a lie; the huge number of disrupted adoptions speaks to this fact. The latter is a destructive insult that justifies the societal trend to disenfranchise parents from raising their own children all together.

It is true that some adoptive parents may have the next Dave Thomas or Faith Hill on their hands. But it is just as likely, particularly if they are adopting older children, that parents may have the next David Berkowitz (abused and adopted) or Charles Manson on their hands (abused and in foster care). There are no statistics to quote, but from my experience I estimate that about 20% of the children who come into care are fairly healthy with few developmental problems. These children look normal and need little to no extraordinary interventions. About 60% of the children who come into care exhibit moderate developmental problems and could probably succeed with effective treatment interventions and parenting behaviors. The other 20% of the children who come into care are deeply disturbed and it is unlikely they will ever function in a family or in society without extreme measures.

Statistics show foster children are more likely than non-foster children to become truants, school dropouts, substance abusers, criminals, incarcerated, pregnant as teenagers, and have out-of-wedlock births. These data suggest several conclusions: (1) genetics are powerful indicators of adult outcomes because foster children turn out more like their birth families than their adopted families, (2) early environments are powerful indicators of adult outcomes because foster children are more likely to have been exposed to trauma during their early childhoods than non-foster children, (3) the foster care system is doing children no good.

The last conclusion is an easy target, but in their defense one must consider that the two previous conclusions are true as well: children have genetic predispositions that can be triggered by and exasperated by trauma, and continued exposure to trauma causes a variety of learning and behavioral difficulties. Therefore, these children came into the social service system already severely maladapted to familial and societal expectations. What doesn't help, is that most are placed in home environments sorely lacking in information and skill on how to live with and raise traumatized children, and effective services to support these families are for the most part not available.

The foster care system, like most systems that serve children, is antiquated, misguided, and dysfunctional. It began with the best of intentions but has changed little in accordance with what we now know about child development and family life. It's not entirely the fault of the system because it is wedded to the judicial system, which does not place children's rights above adult's rights.

Foster parenting itself is probably the most misunderstood and misguided aspect of the system. In an attempt to normalize a traumatized child's experience of being removed from his birth family, he is placed with strangers to act as his surrogate family, and they are expected to nurture him, but not to get attached to him. They are also expected to risk their way of life on some unknown factor who will disrupt their lives, challenge every parenting thought they ever had, traumatize them (what Foster Cline calls the "importing of pathology" into the foster/adoptive home), and place them and their reputations in precarious situations if he falsely accuses them of abuse or if his accidents bring about an investigation, charges, and revocation of their license (which happens much more often than you think because foster parents are held to an outrageously high standard compared to birth parents). They are asked to do this with little compensation or support.

I know many dedicated administrators and social workers who are working towards changing the system in their counties and states, but it is slow going. The following are a few suggestions I have for best practice regarding prevention of childhood trauma and interventions once it has occurred, as well as the changing role of foster parents.

Primary Prevention

Child Development and Parenting courses should be mandatory in middle school and again in high school (these age groups have different developmental capacities and will respond to the materials presented at different times in different ways). These courses should include education and practical experiences that demonstrate cost of living, appropriate infant and childcare, and information on the devastating and lifelong effects of abuse and neglect on child development. These courses should stress the societal expectation that parents are completely responsible for raising their own children (not the village! although, parents should absolutely ask the village for advice and guidance). Not only are parents responsible for raising their own children, but also are to do so by using acceptable parenting practices (within a normal range).

Intervention

1) When parents do not fulfill their responsibilities, Social Services should respond with a variety of services that can be implemented while the child remains in the care of her birth parents. For example, some states have adopted a multiple response system (MRS) to answer calls of abuse and neglect. MRS allows many children to remain in their homes if they are not in imminent danger. Social services immediately flood the family with crisis interventions such

as in-home parent coaching, community resources (food, clothes, taxi services, job opportunities, drug and alcohol or domestic violence counseling) and support (clergy and lay counselors). In addition, there are programs like Family Foster Care in which the family in crisis (parent and children) moves in with a foster family. The foster family provides support, modeling, and coaching to the crisis family for several months, assisting them in getting back on their feet, and adapting more effective parenting skills.

2) When parents are unable or unwilling to respond to these interventions, children should be placed in foster care while their parents continue to receive a variety of services over a six-month period. Because many parents whose children come into foster care were often traumatized themselves as children, we should expect they would have difficulty completing their treatment plans on their own. These parents should be assigned their own Guardian ad Litem (GAL) or assistant, such as a mentor parent who has already successfully completed the program. Failure to comply with the service plan within the six-month period (given that they have a support person) is grounds to proceed with termination of parental rights. Given this plan (six months of services while the child resides in the home and six months of services while the child is in care), a child should be returned home within six months of removal. If she does not return home during that time, we should be quite confident that she would probably never return.

3) All children coming into the system deserve a complete assessment/evaluation of their emotional development along with the physical and mental profiles that are sometimes provided. This information is necessary in making decisions regarding the level of out-of-home care

that is required for a particular child and what the birth parents need to know about raising this child. All reports should be made available to all interested parties, including the birth parents and the foster parents.

4) Infants and toddlers coming into the system should have daily visitation with their birth parents. Visitation should include parent coaching and regular assessments of the parent-child relationship with feedback to the parents. If parents cannot maintain this level of contact and provide suitable interactions, visitation should cease and termination pursued. Infants and toddlers should not be moved for the first three years of their lives unless it is to move home with their birth parents, or if it is proven they are in an unfit foster environment.

5) Foster care should be short term. Any longer than six months is expecting too much from many foster parents (not to mention the child) who, if they are emotionally healthy, may fall in love with the child and may want to adopt the child. At this point the system becomes compromised because the foster parent's goals have changed. This is not necessarily a bad thing unless the child is not going to be available for adoption. For foster care to be short term, the appeal process must change. Birth parents have the right to appeal termination of their parental rights. The appeal process, though, can take years. I believe that if birth parents cannot make their case the first time around they should have to pay a percentage of the court costs to appeal the decision. Even a small percentage, say 10%, would do. I predict that as many as 75% percent of those parents who would have appealed on a free ticket of your and my taxes, would not make the effort if they had to pay for a second chance. This small step could free-up precious court time, save the courts hundreds of thousands

of dollars every year, and insure children permanency within a reasonable time period.

In addition, spending months and years seeking out a birth father who did not know or doesn't care that he has a child is a colossal waste of time. It is no surprise to anyone that having sex can result in pregnancy and the birth of a child. Men need to make efforts to know whether their sexual activities have produced children; it is not up to the state to keep track of their sperm. Not knowing that they have children, or knowing but not being involved in their children's lives from the beginning is neglect, and should be grounds enough to terminate their parental rights. And a man cannot claim that the mother would not let him see his child. He can still demonstrate involvement with the all mighty dollar. If men and women choose sexual freedom (sex without legal commitment), then they shouldn't come crying to the state about their legal rights over "their" children.

6) Speaking of insurances for children, this country needs to establish a bill of rights for children that protects them from their parents while at the same time does not usurp parental power in raising their own children. I know it sounds impossible, but I have faith that we can figure this one out.

7) Therapeutic interventions need to match the urgency with which we expect social services to respond. Human beings are children for only 20% of their lives. The other 80% is spent as adults. Research suggests that the resources and interventions we put in place in childhood can significantly impact future outcomes, for those in care as well as for those yet to come (their children). But I have seen children whose futures were put on hold because judges played musical chairs, or because criminal court

took precedence over family court. I have seen children whose interventions were put on hold while agencies argued over who would pay the bill; children who were provided inadequate services because an agency was unwilling to give up "ownership" of the child, or was only willing to piece-meal together services it provides; and children neglected or put off for so long that the prison system took over the responsibility of providing services, such as they were.

Changing Role of Foster Parents

1) Very few children entering foster care will transition smoothly into a traditional, two-parents working sort of foster home. The majority (not just those who are medically fragile) will require parents with far more training and availability. Therefore, foster parents should not be fostering on the side while they have another job; foster parenting is their job. They should be well trained (making the distinction between foster parents and therapeutic foster parents obsolete), and well paid so they can provide full time care for each child (this would include home-schooling if the child can not function in a school environment). As part of their full time position, foster parents should be present at every court date and every team meeting - they should function like the GAL, not the child's perspective adoptive parent. The foster parent's first goal is to support and promote reunification with the birth family. They should be responsible for co-supervising visits and facilitating the birth parent-child relationship. And, they should be involved in the child's therapy, if needed, as should the birth parents.

Final Word

Society needs to know that raising foster/adopted children is hard work, much more so than raising typical birth children; viewing children in care as if they are no different from children in birth families does them a great disservice, and places society in great jeopardy. We all need to be committed and well informed with eyes wide open. Expectations must be adjusted, and support and training provided throughout a traumatized child's development. Love may be enough for some children, but for many traumatized children it won't even come close.

References

Ainsworth, M. D. (1973). The Development of Infant-Mother Attachment. In B. M. Caldwell and H. N. Ricciuti (Eds.) Review of Child Development Research, Vol. 3. Chicago, IL: University of Chicago Press.

Ainsworth, M. D. (1989). Attachments Beyond Infancy. American Psychologist, 44, 709-716.

Amato, P.R. (1990). Dimensions of the Family Environment as Perceived by Children: A Multidimensional Scaling Analysis. Journal of Marriage and the Family, 52, 613-620.

Berscheid, E., Snyder, M., Omoto, A.M. (1989). The Relationship Closeness Inventory: Assessing the Closeness of Interpersonal Relationships. Journal of Personality and Social Psychology, 57, 792-807.

Bettelheim, B. (1950). Love Is Not Enough. Glencoe, IL: The Free Press.

Bolton, F.G., (1983). When Attachment Fails: Clinical Assessment of High-Risk Families. Beverly Hills, CA: Sage Publications.

Bretherton, I. (1992). The \Origins of Attachment Theory: John Bowlby and Mary Ainsworth. Developmental Psychology, 28, 759-775.

Brody, G.H., & Shaffer, D.R. (1982). Contributions of Parents and Peers to Children's Moral Development. Developmental Review, 2, 31-75.

Cline, F. (1979). Understanding and Treating the Severely Disturbed Child. Evergreen, CO: EC Publications.

Crittendon, P.M. & Claussen, A.H. (2000). The Organiza tion of Attachment Relationships. Cambridge, MA: University Press.

Crockenberg, Jackson, & Langrock, (1996). Autonomy and Goal Attainment: Parenting, Gender, and Children's Social Competence. In M. Killen (Ed.) New Directions in Child Development # 73. San Francisco: Jossey-Bass Publishers.

Darling, N., & Steinberg, L. (1993). Parenting Style as Context: An Integrative Model. Psychological Bulletin, 113, 487-496.

Eisenberg, & Mussen, (1989). The Roots of Prosocial Behavior in Children. Cambridge, England: Cambridge Press

Erikson, E. (1963). Childhood and Society (2nd ed.). NY: Norton.

Fonagy, P. (2001). The Human Genome and the Representational World: The Role of Early Mother-Infant Interaction in Creating an Interpersonal Interpretive Mechanism. Bulletin of The Menninger Clinic, 65 (3), pp. 427 - 448.

Gacono, C.B. and Meloy, J.R. (1994). The Rorschach Assessment of Aggressive and Psychopathic Personalities. Hillsdale, New Jersey: Lawrence Erlbaum Associates.

Gilligan, J. (1999). Violent Offenders: What Went Wrong Developmentally? Presentation at the Violence in Children, Adolescents, and Families: Strategies for Prevention and Clinical Intervention, First annual course from The Consolidated Department of Psychiatry, Harvard Medical School.

Federici, R. S. (1998). Help For the Hopeless Child: A Guide For Families. Federici and Associates. Alexandria, VA.

Gottman, J. M., Katz, L. F., & Hooven, C. (1996). Parental Meta-Emotion Philosophy and the Emotional Life of Families: Theoretical Models and Preliminary Data. Journal of Family Psychology, 10, 243-268.

Hinde, R.A., & Stevenson-Hinde, J. (1987). Interpersonal Relationships and Child Development. Developmental Review, 7, 1-21.

Hinde, R.A., & Stevenson-Hinde, J. (1988). Relationships Within Families: Mutual influences. Oxford: Clarendon Press.

James, B. (1994). A Brief Treatise on Coercive Holding. Handbook for Treatment of Attachment-Trauma Problems in Children. Lexington, MA: Lexington Books.

Kohut, H. (1971). The Analysis of the Self. New York, NY: International Universities Press.

Latham, C. (1999) Treatment of Sexually Abusive Children. Presentation at the Violence in Children, Adolescents, and Families: Strategies for Prevention and Clinical Intervention, First annual course from The Consolidated Department of Psychiatry, Harvard Medical School.

Lewis, M., & M.W. Sullivan (1994). Design and Evaluation of Developmental Interventions. In C.B. Fisher, & R.M. Lerner (Eds.) Applied Developmental Psychology. NY, NY: Mcgraw-Hill

Maccoby, E.E. (1992). The Role of Parents in the Socializa tion of Children: An Historical Overview. Developmental Psychology, 28, 1006 -1017.

Maccoby, E.E., & Martin, J.A. (1983). Socialization in the Context of the Family: Parent-Child Interaction. In P.H. Mussen (Series Ed.) & E.M.

Main, M., & George, C., (1985). Responses of Abused and Disadvantaged Toddlers to Distress in Agemates: A study in the day care setting. Developmental Psychology, 21:3, 407-412

Perry, B. (1995). Incubated in Terror: Neurodevelopment in the Cycle of Violence. Children Youth and Violence: Searching for Solutions. New York, NY: The Guilford Press.

Porges, Stephen W., (2003). Social Engagement and Attachment: A Phylogentic Perspective. Brain-Body Center. Dept. of Psychiatry University of IL at Chicago.

Postman, N. (1994). The Disappearance of Childhood. New York, NY: Vintage Books.

Power, M.B., & Krause, E.B. (1995). Adoption, Myth, and Emotion Work: Paths to Disillusionment. In M.G. Flaherty (Ed.) Social Perspectives on Emotion. Vol. 3 (97-120). Greenwich, CT: Jai Press, Inc.

Randolph. E. (2001). Broken Hearts; Wounded Minds. Evergreen, CO: RFR Publications

Rapoport, J.L., & Ismond, D.R. (1996). The DSM-IV Training Guide For Diagnosis of Childhood Disorders. Philadelphia, PA: Brunner/Mazel

Richters, M.M., & Volkmar, F.R. (1994). Reactive Attachment Disorder of Infancy or Early Childhood. Journal of the American Academy of Child and Adolescent Psychiatry. Vol 33 (3).

Rygaard, N. (1998) Attachment Disorder/Psychopathic Development in Children. Tele Denmark site www.sitecenter.dk/www.npr-attachment.dk

Sagi, A., & Hoffman, M.L. (1976). Empathic Distress in the Newborn. Developmental Psychology. Mar. Vol. 12 (2) 175-176.

Thompson, R. F. (1993). The Brain: A Neuroscience Primer. New York, NY: W.H. Freeman and Company

van Gulden, H. & Riedel, C. (2000). In Search Of Self: Reclaiming andHealing the Lost, Wounded, and Missing Parts of Self. (manuscript). Minneapolis, MN: Adoptive Family Counseling Center

van Ijzendoorn, M.H. & Bakermans-Kranenburk, M.J. (1996). Attachment Representations in Mothers, Fathers, Adolescents, and Clinical Groups: A Meta-Analytic Search for Normative Data.

Vygotsky, L. S. (1978). Mind in society: The Development of Higher Psychological Processes. Cambridge, MA: Harvard University Press.

Youniss, J. (1980). Parents and Peers in Social Development. The University of Chicago Press: Chicago, IL.

Additional Readings

Adopting The Hurt Child (1995). Keck, G., & Kupecky, R. Colorado Springs, CO: Pinon Press

Abusive Relationships, Care and Control Conflicts and Insecure Attachments (2001). Peter Reder & Sylvia Duncan. Child Abuse Review Vol. 10: 411-427.

Assessing Adult Attachment: Interview Course with Patricia Crittenden (2001). Child Abuse Review Vol. 10: 440-447.

Attachment Theory and Psychoanalysis (2001). Fonagy, P. New York, NY: Other Press

Attachment Theory and Child Abuse: An Overview of the Literature for Practitioners (2001). Heather Bacon & Sue Richardson. Child Abuse Review Vol. 10: 377-

397.

Attachment Theory: Social, Developmental, and Clinical
Perspectives (1995). S. Goldberg, R. Muir and J.
Kerr (Eds.) Hillsdale, NJ: The Analytic Press.

Attachment, Trauma, and Healing (1998) Levy, T. &
Orlans, M. Washington, DC: CWLA Press

Autonomy and the Personal: Negotiation and Social
Reciprocity (1996). Nucci, L. P., Killen, M., Smetna,
J. G., In M. Killen (Ed.)

Children's Autonomy, Social Competence, and Interactions
With Adults and Other Children: Exploring
Connections and Consequences, # 73. San Francisco:
Jossey-Bass Publishers.

Building the Bonds of Attachment: Awakening Love in
Deeply Troubled Children. (1998). Daniel
Hughes. Jason Arson Inc.

Creative Responses to Child Sexual Abuse (2001). S.
Richardson and H. Bacon (Eds.) United Kingdom:
Kingsley Publishers

Emotional Development: The Organization of Emotional
Life in the Early Years (1997). Alan Stroufe.
Cambridge University Press

Ghosts From The Nursery (1997) Karr-Morse, R. & Wiley,
M. S. New York, NY: The Atlantic Monthly Press

Human Attachment (1996). Colin, V., Philadelphia, PA:
Temple University Press

Learning To Love: Mechanisms and Milestones (1991).
Waters, E.,Kondo-Ikemura, K., Richters, J.E.,
Posada, G. In. M. Gunner and A. Sroufe
(Eds.) Minnesota Symposium on Child Psychology.
Vol. 23 (217-255).

Reactive Attachment Disorder: What We Know About The Disorder And Implications For Treatment (2000) Hanson, R.F. & Spratt, E.G. (2000). Child Maltreatment, Vol. 5, No. 2, (137-145).

Recent Research on Adoption, Attachment and Related Fields (1999, 2003). Sally Popper. Crittenton Center for Child and Family Development. Kansas City, MO.

The Effects of Early Relational Trauma on Right Brain Development, Affect Regulation, and Infant Mental Health (2001). A. N. Schore. Infant Mental Health, 22 (1-2),

Violent Attachments (1992). Meloy, J.R. Northvale, NJ: Jason Aronson Inc.

Appendix A

Parent-Child Relationships Amongst
The Traumatized Child Population

This survey tool was designed to help foster and adoptive families better understand their relationships with their traumatized child(ren). It suggests concrete stop and start behaviors and represents a spectrum of children's relationship issues (e.g., a plethora of negative behaviors and a paucity of positive behaviors). This tool can also be used as a resource in developing parenting and therapeutic treatment plans for children and families.

If you feel uncomfortable during or after filling out this survey or are unsure as to how to use it to benefit your family, please contact me at (919) 542-2037. Or if you have any questions contact me or visit my web site at www.brandnewdayconsulting.com

If you are willing for your responses to be used for further research, please send a copy of your completed survey to:

Katharine Leslie, Ph.D.
250 Silene Dr.
Pittsboro, NC 27312
kpleslie@att.net

All responses should be anonymous. Please do not include your name or the names of your children when submitting a copy of your survey. Results of any further research will be used to educate social service and mental health professionals, law makers, and the general public.

The survey contains a list of positive and negative child behaviors and attitudes. Please circle or put a check mark next to the behaviors that apply to a particular child in your care. If you have more than one child you can use the same survey tool by using a color code system (e.g., red pen for John, blue pen for Susie). Mothers and fathers should each fill out a survey independently.

Shares My Values

Understands that you have to work hard for what you want
Loves life
Loves the lord
Loves her/himself
Thinks home is her favorite place
Enjoys family celebrations
Wants to know family history
Adds to family unity and peacefulness
Likes spending time with the family
Is loving towards siblings
Enjoys going to school
Wants to do what is right
Compassionate and loving towards pets
Good friend to others
Gets along well with others
Kind and giving to others
Caring of other's feelings
Friends and relationships are important
Is polite to other adults
Accepts differences among people
Grateful and appreciative of things and lessons
Is remorseful when he/she makes a mistake
Stands up for her/himself
Makes the best of a bad situation

Elicits Positive Attention From Me

Wants me to share in his/her successes
Shares what he/she is proud of
Can't wait to tell me something that he/she learned or saw
Wants me to watch him/her play
Asks for attention and strokes
Wants to please me and hates it when he/she disappoints me
Demonstrates behavior we've talked about
Copies my positive behaviors
Learns from me, tries to imitate me
Tries to do the things I nag about
Responds respectfully to my discipline
Acknowledges that I am speaking to him
Helps out with daily tasks without a battle
Does things to help me
Listens to me and follows my directions
Appreciates my efforts

Makes Me Feel Needed

Is excited to see me at the end of the day
Runs to me when I pick him/her up after a separation
Twinkle (love) in his/her eyes when he/she sees me
Feels sad when I leave
Looks to me for comfort
Lets me teach him/her things
Needs me to kiss his/her booboos
Enjoys having me involved with sporting events and activities
Wants to share things with me
Seeks me out when he/she is scared or hurt
Is comforted by being with me

Sincerely Makes Me Feel Special

Gives me support
Encourages me through tough times
Shows concern when I am upset
Loves me even on my bad days
Asks me if I need help

Pays attention to me
Compliments me
Seems to like me
Expresses love and care to me
Talks about me to others in a positive way
Tells me I'm the best Mommy/Daddy
Tells me I am the most important person in his/her life
Tells me I'm great
Tells me new ways he/she loves me
Wants one-on-one time with me
Won't go to bed without a story from me
Rather be with me than anyone else
Rather play a game with me than watch TV
Wants to be close to me

Demonstrates Trust In Me

Comes to me when he/she has a nightmare
Asks for help
Comes to me for a hug after being scolded
Lays on me when he/she is sick
Falls asleep in my arms
Comes to me for advice
Looks up to me
Wants my opinion about his/her life
Talks to me about his/her problems
Listens to my life stories
Comes to me for answers
Feels free to talk to me
Shares the good and the bad
Lets me give him/her hugs and kisses
Talks to me about almost everything
Tells me his/her fears
Talks to me with honesty
Cares about what I think
Knows I will be there

Is Fun to Be Around

Enjoy activities together
Asks me to play with him/her
Plays, teases, and jokes around with me
We talk, play, and share feelings with each other
We cuddle together
She/he loves my laughing at her/him
We wrestle together
Talk together about life
We read together
He/she plays freely with me
Has fun with me
We love being near each other
Her/his kisses make me laugh
Laughs at funny things I do
Laughs with me

Expresses Love and Affection

Gives me unconditional love
Gives me hugs and kisses every day
Isn't afraid to show me love
Freely tells me he/she loves me
Loves to tell me he/she loves me
Responds to affection with warmth and happiness
Hugs and kisses me spontaneously
Smiles back at me many times a day
Hugs my neck
Smells my hair like it's a flower
Kisses and hugs me over and over just to say goodbye
Writes me cards to tell me he/she loves me

Negative Behaviors and Attitudes

Chatters incessantly
Makes noise incessantly
Asks a lot of nonsense questions
Mumbles under breath
Lies to stay out of trouble
Lies for no apparent reason
Doesn't learn from past
Pits adults against each other
Hyper vigilant
Steals
Cheats
Picks at scabs, cuts self
Falls and trips on purpose
Talks like a baby
Will not follow rules to games
Resists comfort and nurturing
Clingy at the wrong times
Inauthentic (phony)
Poor eye contact
Cruel to animals
Oppositional/defiant
Self-important
Know-it-all
Lethargic/lazy
Mistrustful (nosey)
Overly anxious
Overly dependent
Overly self-protective
Whiny
Inconsolable
Manipulative
Irresponsible
Shallow
Indifferent
Controlling
Callous
Narcissistic

Parasitic
Violent
Dramatic
Disorganized
Socially inept
Aggressive
Rigid
Ask questions he/she already knows the answers to
Consequences/punishments have no effect on behavior
Throws objects, punches and kicks things and/or people
Asks for help when not needed and doesn't ask for help
    when needed
Demands attention, especially when another child is
    receiving attention
Presumes entitlement (I am KING and you are here to
    serve me)
Envious (thinks everyone else has more than him/her)
Gives little or nothing of him/herself to parents or others
Shows no mastery in game playing or in creating anything
Poor peer relationships (children of the same age)
Bottomless pit that sucks everything out of you
Excessive fit throwing for prolonged periods of time
No stable sense of self (chameleon like)
Vacillates between anger and helplessness
Needs constant attention/approval
Lacks expressiveness (low or flat affect)
Avoids eye contact except when lying
Doesn't learn from discipline or punishment
Unreceptive to teaching/guiding/coaching
Interprets other's intensions defensively
Uses verbal or physical intimidation
Destroys own stuff including toys and clothes
Destroys the property of others
Won't brush teeth, shower, or clean him/herself
Too affectionate and engaging with adults
Not sincerely affectionate with parents
Won't share, but expects others to share
Argumentative and contrary
Overly Independent (pseudo)

Takes a lot of negative risks
Easily triggered frustration
Rejects food from caregiver
Unreceptive to parental advice
Unreceptive to parental discipline
Negative behaviors do not change
Never sincerely sorry for wrong doing
Urinates outside of the toilet
Defecates outside of the toilet
Sexually acts out on self
Sexually acts out on others

The child I am thinking about when filling out this survey:

is my Birth/Foster/Adopted child (circle one) and is
_____ years old,

and has lived with me for (months, years)
_____.

I would rate my relationship satisfaction with this child as:

very   somewhat   somewhat
          very
unsatisfying   **un**satisfying   satisfying   satisfying

Circle the statement that is most true

> I love this child a lot
> I somewhat love this child
> I do not love this child at all

Circle the statement that is most true

> I like this child a lot.
> I somewhat like this child.
> I do not like this child at all.

How much joy do you feel (receive) parenting this child?

> none   a little   more then a little
> a lot   tons